Cricut for Beginners

A Step-By-Step Guide To Master Your Cricut Machine And Design Space and Make Money With It.

How To Start a Business With Cricut. Can You Make It?

Tips and Tricks Included.

Jennifer Tuffin

Table of Contents

Introduction

With all the major adjustments that have happened in 2020, what we once perceived as our normal lifestyle has now been greatly altered. As many working from home and many of us needing that second or third stream of income, we all have to put our minds to use and come up with creative ways to stay afloat financially. It's estimated that about 25-30% of the workforce in the United States alone, will be working from home for multiple days a week by the end of 2021 (Work-At-Home After Covid 19, n.d.).

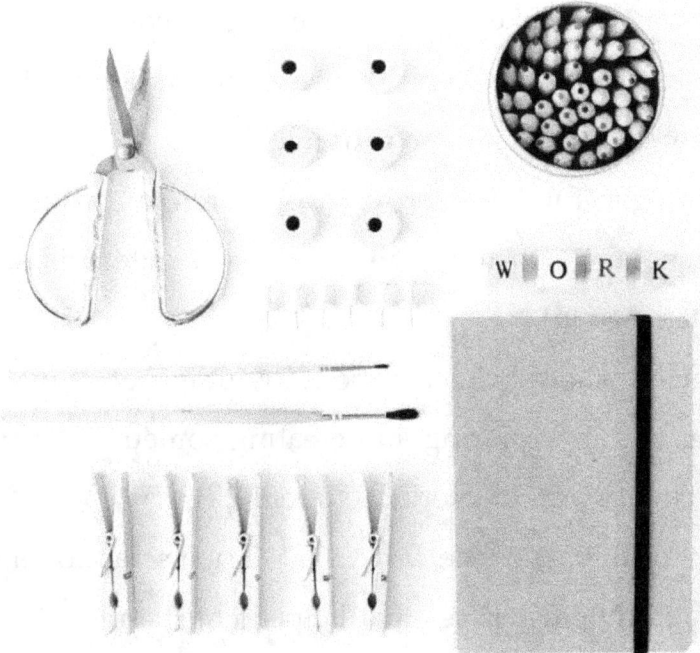

With this estimation forecasting the next few months, in addition to the current lifestyle that we're all living, it's easy to predict that working from home may just be the new norm for a lot of us! However, side-hustles (from home) don't have to be a bore nor do they have to be draining. They can be businesses that merely develop from our interest in other fields or industries, and this is the exact direction that a lot of people took when looking for their second stream of income.

Because most of us were forced to stay at home during most of 2020, there was much more time for us to explore our hobbies and interests; and thus, evolve those hobbies and interests into skill sets, and then into streams of income!

This was clearly prominent on social media apps such as Tik Tok, where people would market their small craft businesses and direct users to their "link in bio" (which was usually to their website or a site like Etsy), and within months, their small business was churning in thousands of dollars!

Thankfully, an amazing company by the name of 'Cricut' was there for many of us during 2020. The company offered a way to keep us fellow creatives busy, explore our hobbies, *and* find ways to make a second stream of income from our own homes! It offered many people a means of turning their arts and crafts projects into full-blown businesses that are now self-sufficient and thriving.

And judging by the general forecast of work trends, many are following in entrepreneurs' footsteps and starting their own small enterprises, especially within fields that they are interested in.

The one prominently fantastic factor about Cricut is that its machines offer exactly that service—assisting you in exploring and creating something that you're interested in, and then making them as gifts or products to sell!

Cricut has been around since the early 2000s when scrapbooking was growing in popularity. They created little machines that helped cut the most beautiful designs out of paper and tissue paper, to decorate the pages of our scrapbooks.

Since then, Cricut evolved their machines into full-blown powerhouse machines that are every creative's dream machine! Cricut's range of machines can now tackle hundreds of materials such as vinyl, foil, wood, paper, card stock, fabric, leather, and chipboard! They've made their range of machines suitable for absolutely anyone interested in exploring their creative side.

What makes the Cricut range more fascinating is that their range of machines now work hand-in-hand with their own software known as "Design Space," where you can choose, create or alter images to make your own digital designs, then use your Cricut machine to cut, draw, print, etch, deboss or write it!

Now that we have been requested to stay at home more, this works perfectly with our ability to explore our hobbies and find other forms of side hustles. Considering the capabilities and versatility of the Cricut range, using a Cricut machine to start a side hustle by making your favorite projects may just be a completely viable option!

Most of the world was forced to work from home and online. Thanks to the internet, we were able to not only *shop* online but also to find work online. Many sought after this opportunity and grabbed it with both hands, turning their side hustles into their full-time jobs! With many more small business owners running self-sufficient careers, the possibility of running your own business or side hustle has become much more possible and promising.

In *Cricut for Beginners*, we will be exploring the entire world of Cricut— maneuvering through Design Space's interface, understanding key terminology related to the machines, what tools you need for different materials and projects, and most importantly, how to make money from your machine! We're going to look at how to turn the purchase of your Cricut machine into an investment for your future!

Cricut has been refining the perfection of what it means to be an "all-in-one" machine, by combining technology, arts and crafts, and business into one system and machine to help you (and motivate you to) explore your creative side whilst expanding your skillset *and* starting a business for yourself.

With all the possibilities at our literal fingertips, let's dive right into what Cricut can offer us and get started on our Cricuting journey!

Chapter 1: The World of Cricut

The world of Cricutting began in 2003 as a quirky little tool to help ease the process of and explore cutting patterns for different sorts of papers for scrapbooking (Take a Look at the Evolution of Cricut Machines, n.d.).

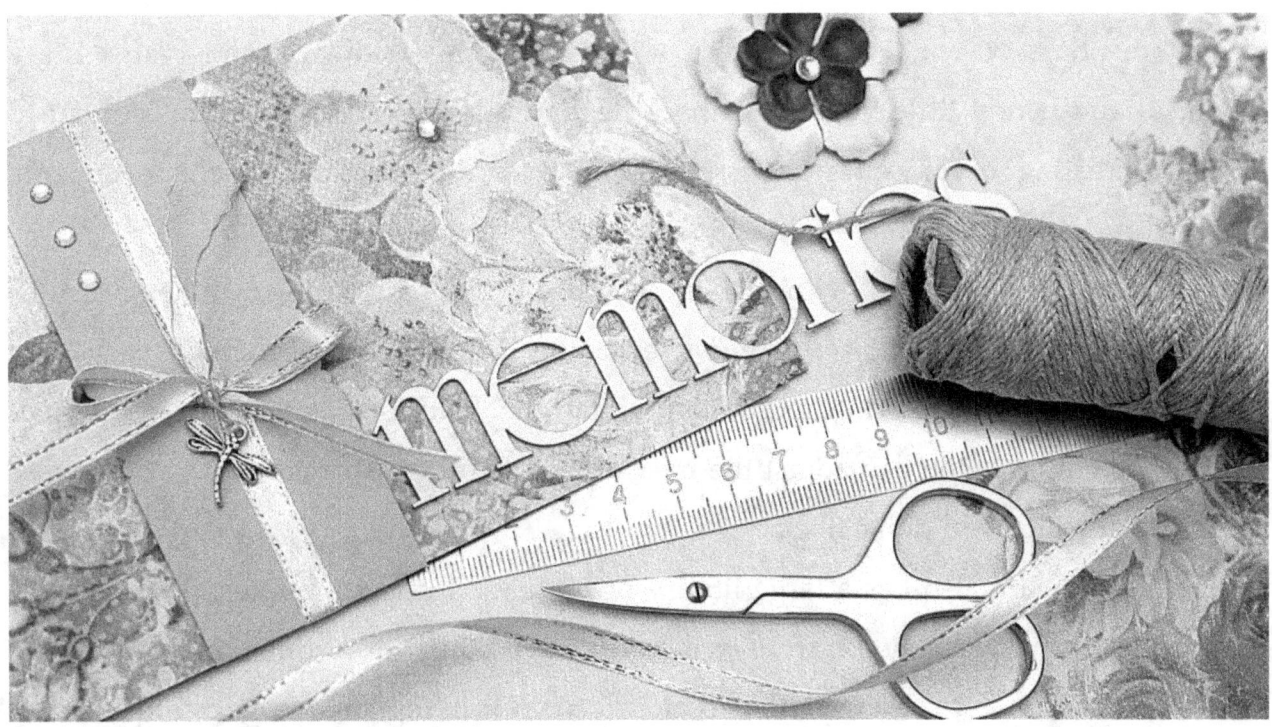

Started by the company *Provo Craft & Novelty, Inc.* in Utah, the company solely manufactures and expands that vast range of Cricut machines, tools, and materials that we now have today, and it's only getting better!

What once started as a mere tool to help explore our arts and crafts hobby has now become a full-blown franchise, with powerful machines and tools that can help us not only further explore our creative side, but also make the most gorgeous gifts, decorations, and products to sell.

Cricut machines have become a machine that's not only efficient in helping us cut beautiful designs and patterns into materials, it has also diversified in terms of the materials that we can use to create and customize. It became such a popular tool that Cricut teamed up with the renowned cooking show host, Martha Stewart to make a range for baking.

Nowadays, Cricut isn't simply a tool for helping with arts and crafts, it's a powerful and handy little household machine, and at the very least, an investment to save on creating decór, gifts and starting up a side-line hustle to create custom, personalized products with your machine!

Cricut machines work with specific software designed for the machine known as "Cricut Design Space." The software is free with all devices and essentially acts as a 'canvas' in a way, where you choose images, designs, texts, or patterns for your Cricut machine to cut out. You can adjust the measurements on the software and also choose the material which you'd like to cut.

The software also has a large library of preloaded images, quotes, patterns, and project ideas for you to choose from (which can save you a lot of time), or you can use those preloaded stock as a template and alter it to your liking, or simply create a design or patterns from scratch.

In terms of machinery, there are a few options to choose from and while all of the machines can cut simpler materials such as paper, vinyl, and fabric, you may want to look at the newer models if you'd like to explore etchings or require a faster machine for more efficiency in production time. The newer ranges are also more versatile in the materials that it can cut, for instance, thin cork can also be cut.

The **Cricut Personal machine** is the one that started it all, back in 2003. This model didn't need a software program and it was quite limited with cutting design options — everything was built into the system and you chose patterns from the on-screen options on the machine. The Personal can only cut 5.5 x 11 inches and smaller and could only take cutting mats with a width of 6 inches, so if you are looking for something simple and easy to use, specifically to cut smaller designs with easy-to-cut materials then the Cricut Personal can be a great and affordable option for you (Cricut History, 2020).

The **Cricut Create** came next and was also known as "Provo Craft" back then. Although the Create was the same size as the Personal, there were a few improvements such as an update in the display screen, tech, and design features. The Create also came with an 8-way directional blade and came in different colors.

After the Create, the **Expression range** was launched (the Expression 1 and the Expression 2). This range came with significant changes, such as a 12 x 24" cutting ability, better precision with smaller cuts as well as the ability to tackle more materials such as poster board and vellum. The development of the precursor to Cricut Design Space was Cricut Craft Room, and it made its mark in software development for the Cricut machines and their capabilities. The Cricut Craft Room was able to work hand-in-hand with the Expression range, however, the Expression 1 could still also be used as a standalone machine. The Expression 2 is still a considerably popular machine and naturally, was an improvement from the Expression 1 with *major* changes.

For starters, the machine was larger, faster, and came with a full-color screen. There were also around 200+ preloaded designs, fonts, images, patterns, and more, as well as more options for design alterations (such as resizing, rotations, flipping, mirroring). The Expression 2 is a great and affordable machine for those who want to tackle smaller projects while also learning to work with Design Space or Craft Room.

Thereafter, the **Cricut EasyPress Mini** was launched. It was a considerably small machine that was great for travel purposes or for those that want to explore the world of Cricutting, but with limited working space. The Mini was the first machine that needed a computer with software to function. The Mini also has a smaller cutting width of 8.5" so it can only tackle much smaller designs and cuts, and much lighter materials such as paper and fabric.

The **Cricut Cake Machine** was next in line, and part of the **Cricut Martha Stewart Range**. It was used specifically for assisting with decorating baked goods such as cakes, cookies, and cupcakes.

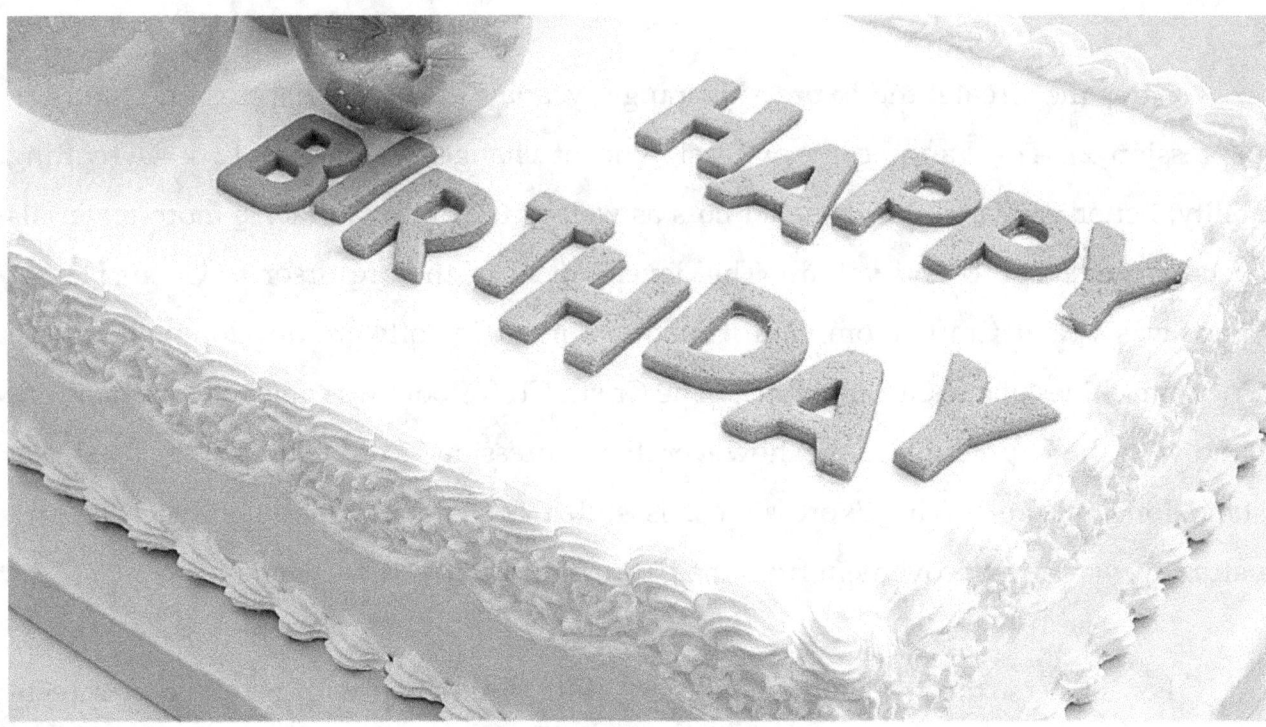

The Cake Machine works with materials such as fondant, frosting sheets, gum paste, etc. It's best for those who want to work primarily in baking or cake decorating, otherwise, it would hardly be used for those who bake or decorate cakes every once in a while. The Cake Machine is designed for those who bake regularly or can benefit from the efficiency of the Cake Machine's function.

Thereafter, the two most popular and powerful models were launched: the **Explore range** (Explore 1, Explore Air, and Explore 2) as well as the Maker. The Explore 1 has a more modern look to it (this aesthetic is carried all the way through to the Maker model). These models consist of thousands of designs in the Cricut Image Library in the Cricut Design Space and can tackle various materials and designs. These models can also make use of much more blades and pens for cutting and printing. The Explore range as well as the Maker also work extremely well with the Design Space software and offer a larger variety of images, designs, and patterns to choose from, allowing you to reap a plethora of project ideas and options for customizing projects at your fingertips!

The second-most recent model is the **Maker**. Although it's one of the pricier models out of the Cricut range, it is worth the money in terms of its capabilities and specs. The Maker is much faster at cutting and overall processing. The Maker can also handle more materials and has special blades that are only compatible with the Maker, which opens up many more options for designs, cuts, and projects in general.

Lastly, the most recent model is the **Cricut Joy**. Similar to the Cricut Mini, the Joy is one of the smallest machines in the Cricut range, but still equally as powerful as some of the more recent models of the Cricut range. The Joy is about ¼ of the size of the Maker and Air 2 and can only handle a cutting width of about 4", *however*, the biggest difference is that the Joy can handle longer lengths of material (about 20 feet worth of material) than any other Cricut model. The Joy is a fantastic option for those who love to explore smaller projects such as making cards, vinyl or labels with their Cricut machine because even though the machine is tiny, it's still extremely powerful. If you have a smaller working space, the Joy is a fantastic option to consider.

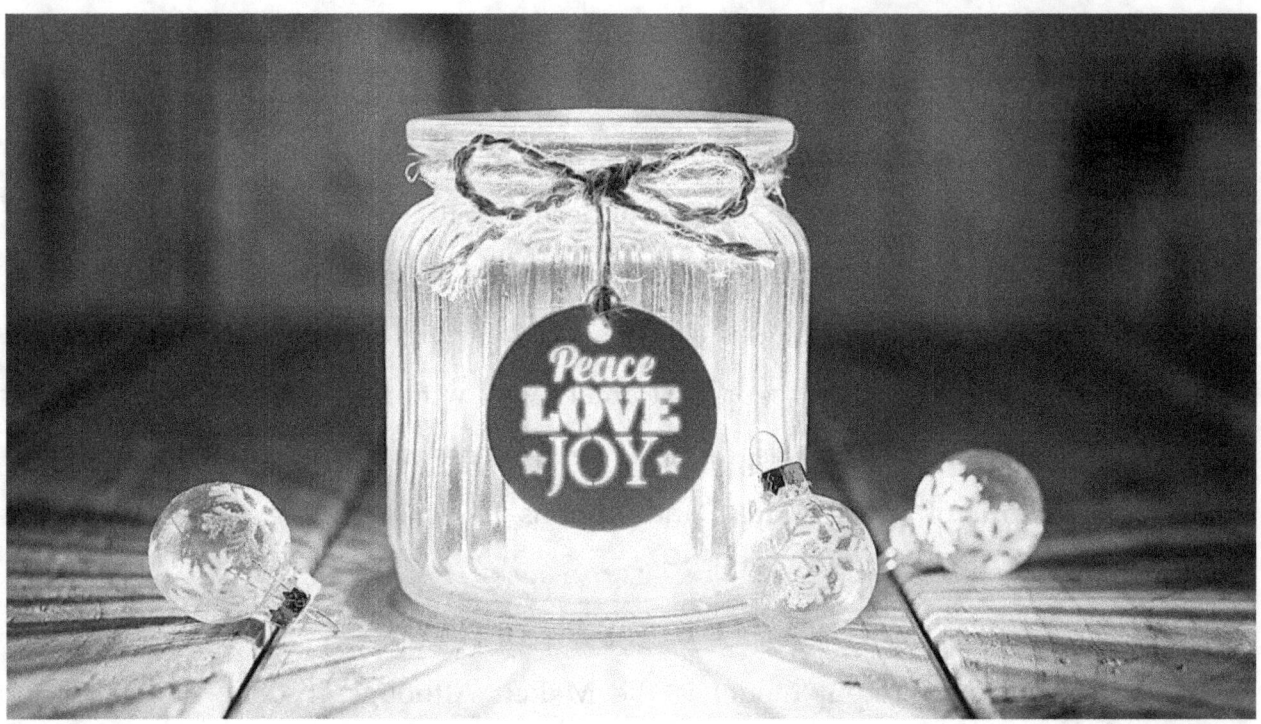

Cricut also has a range of heat tools, called **EasyPress**, which are specifically for pressing delicate materials onto surface areas. It allows you to quickly adjust the heat settings on the machine and can assist in ironing on the designs which you've cut, using your Cricut machine, onto their designated project surfaces in 60 seconds or less! The EasyPress range is fantastic as it's designed specifically to tackle Cricut projects while leaving little to no damage to the design, whereas if you use a normal iron, it may damage the cutout and you'll need to be much more careful when handling the design.

Aside from using budgeting for expenses such as the machine, tools, and materials, to determine what machine you should buy, you can also consider what *type* of projects you'd like to explore. In doing so, you can then determine which machine is best suited for the job. For instance, the Cricut Cake Machine is the model you'd choose to help you explore projects related to baking and cake decorating. The most versatile of machines in the Cricut range is the Maker, so if your budget allows for it, the Maker is an amazing investment!

You can buy your Cricut machine off of their official website, www.cricut.com, where you can also get free shipping nationwide on orders over $99 (Cricut, n.d.). Cricut's website is always offering helpful promo codes to get you the discounts you need, and you can also look out for sales on their homepage. Alternatively, the Cricut community has grown so large in the past few years that you can also look for fellow Cricut bloggers who team up with the company to give other offers on specific machines or tools that they use or access libraries of curated images and designs from them! Although the Cricut Design Space is free, it does offer membership plans for larger libraries of templates, patterns, images, and project ideas for various membership fees that can greatly expand your library! If you follow a few Cricut bloggers online, you can also find specials on some of their libraries.

Membership fees for Design Space are also known as "Cricut Access." These fees are roughly between $8-10 per month or around $100 for a year's membership (Kemp-Gerstel, n.d.). The memberships are categorized as premium, monthly, and annual, and they all come with various benefits.

The first option is the "Premium" option; it's priced at $9.99 per month or $119.88 per year. The Premium membership offers the most benefits, although it is the most expensive option.

All three of the memberships offer 400 fonts and over 75,000 cut-ready images for your perusal and use. The biggest difference with the Premium membership is that you can also get up to 50% savings on other individual licensed fonts, images, and ready-to-make projects. This is only if you ever want to buy an individual project design or template to work with, as there are thousands of options for free (with your membership) on Cricut Access. Premium membership also offers free economy shipping on orders over $50.

Although this may seem a bit pricey on the face-front, it actually benefits Cricutters in the long-run! If you had to purchase an individual project, you may find yourself paying about $1 for a single image and between $3-7 for every "Make It Now" project. Without this, you may find yourself hassling to create designs which takes time and practice, whereas the membership plans not only offer a plethora of fantastic inspiration and ideas, they also offer templates for you to easily and simply bring into Design Space and then head on over to make the project! Grabbing yourself a membership plan saves a lot of unnecessary time, money, and effort in hindsight, making your Cricut process much more efficient while also making the process much less cumbersome.

When you head over to Cricut's website, you can not only shop for your machine, but also various other tools such as blades, pens, and mats, and materials for your projects such as iron-on vinyl and Smart Material (which works exclusively with the Joy). There are also pre-selected base materials such as t-shirts, coasters, bags, and more that you can buy in bulk which can be customized with your Cricut machine. You can also join Cricut Access from the site, for easy set-up and access.

Cricut Machines

The EasyPress 2

The EasyPress 2 isn't necessarily a Cricut cutting machine, but rather a heat-transfer machine that's specifically designed to assist with iron-on vinyl and other decals. Once you've used your Cricut machine to cut your design (with a heat transfer material, such as iron-on), you can then use the EasyPress 2 to help you adhere the design to the designated project surface.

The price of the EasyPress 2 machine is around $189 for the 9x9" and $239 for the 12x12". You can choose between the color options of raspberry, lilac, or mint. The 9x9" is a great option for medium projects such as t-shirts, pillowcases, etc., while the 12x12" option is great for larger projects such as hoodies, blankets, banners, etc. There is also an EasyPress Mini that's going for $69 if you generally want to handle much smaller iron-on designs.

There are also bundle options available when purchasing an EasyPress 2—for $109 you can get an EasyPress Mini with a starter Iron-On kit included, or a 9x9" EasyPress 2 with the starter Iron-On Kit for $209, or the 12x10" EasyPress 2 with the starter Iron-On kit for $259. The starter Iron-On kit has a few colors of iron-on sheets and a weeding toolset (which is used to weed away excess vinyl once the design has been cut). The starter Iron-On bundles are great for if you're starting off and would like to grab a few of the basic tools as well as a selection of iron-ons without paying for each one individually.

Alternatively, Cricut also offers the Everything Iron-On Bundle, which includes the weeding toolset, the essential toolset, and a few Iron-On vinyl along with a few funky colors. The bundle also comes with materials for you to practice with, along with the EasyPress Mini, all for $251,89. There are a few other bundle options such as the Basic Iron-On bundle, but there are various kits that come and go with the seasons.

The Cricut site currently only stocks the most recent machines such as the Maker, Explore Air 2, Joy, and the EasyPress machines. If you are looking for an older model, you may have to hunt down a second-hand one from someone who's selling (and you may be able to grab it at a bargain and can also work in your favor in regard to learning on a cheaper and older model before stepping up to buy a newer, modern model).

The Cricut Maker

The Cricut Maker comes in color options of turquoise blue, lilac, mint, rose or champagne, and is currently priced at around $369. The site also offers bundles where you can grab an Essentials Bundle or an Everything Materials Bundle which includes different varieties of vinyl, pens, mats, and tool kits. The Essentials Bundle goes for around $533.42 while the Everything Bundle goes for around $637.83. However, Cricut was doing a special recently where the Essentials Bundle dropped to an amazing deal of $389.99 and the Everything Bundle was priced just $10 more, at $399.99, so it's worth finding out when Cricut has their holiday sales, clearance sales or promotions, as you can grab a brand-new Maker *and* tool kits, mats, pens, and vinyl for around $200 less than the selling price on their site!

The Cricut Explore Air 2

The Explore Air 2 range also comes in a variety of colors that gorgeously wrap fully around the body of the machine. The color options are blue, mint, lilac, rose, and a neat-looking black. The model is priced at $249.99 and there are also bundle options available such as the Everything Bundle and the Essentials Bundle. The Everything Bundle is going for $487.83 and the Essentials Bundle is going for $383.42.

Lastly, the cute little Joy is priced at $179.99 (which is a much more affordable yet powerful option if you're looking to just specifically dabble with smaller projects such as cards, labels, and small designs). The Joy only comes in a standard blue and white color, and there are a few bundle options available such as the Label Making Bundle, Insert Card Bundle, Smart Vinyl Bundle, Smart Iron-On Bundle, and Essentials Bundle. The bundles vary around the price ranges of $235-$255. Similar to the Maker that has exclusive pens and blades for the machine, the Joy has types of vinyl (known as Smart Iron-Ons) that are created to work seamlessly with the Joy, if you're looking to add vinyl labels or designs to projects.

The Cricut Joy

On the Cricut website, you can also explore the range of tools and materials for the machines on their website, and the tools are categorized into different sections that pertain to the different Cricut models so that you know which tools work with which machines.

Terminology

Cricut Design Space & Cricut Access

First and foremost, the "Cricut Design Space" is one of the tools which you will be using the most. Cricut Design Space is essentially a software that works off of a cloud which essentially acts as a bridge from your templates or whatever you'd like to cut or print, to your Cricut machine and gives it commands on how to go about cutting or printing pieces for your project (Microsoftsurfacedeals, 2016).

The Design Space also works with Cricut Access which is a library of images, designs, templates, patterns, and fonts for texts and quotes so that you can choose and import those that you'd like to incorporate into your project, into the 'canvas' on your design space. The canvas is essentially the main page in Design Space where you will create and alter the final design for your Cricut machine to cut or print. When you import images, etc. from Cricut Access, you'll then adjust it in your canvas so that it fits the measurements of your project surface, and then command your Cricut to start cutting or printing.

Mirror, Weld & Attach

Another important factor to consider when you're in Design Space and about to set up your Cricut machine to cut your design is that you'll need to 'mirror' your designs, especially if they include text. Mirroring is a function in Design Space and it essentially flips your design around so that it's cut the correct way. Most of your HTV projects will require you to mirror your design. If you have shiny HTV, you'll also need to remember to place the shiny side of the vinyl face-down when loading it into the machine.

If you'd like to save on as much material as possible and waste as little as possible, then you can also weld your design on Design Space. In doing so, you're moving the images, letters, or designs as close together as possible so that they touch and are then cut as one big piece rather than individually. If you weld your design, you're not only saving more material but you're also saving the time it takes to cut each piece individually and possibly also having to load the machine multiple times. Welding (meaning 'grouping' items together) needs to be done prior to your pressing cut, and once the design has been cut, you cannot undo the welding if you've saved it as is. If you'd like to keep your images and designs separate for later use, un-weld the items in Design Space after you've cut them, then save the project.

Similar to the Weld function, 'Attach' is another function in Design Space that allows you to keep the images and fonts as they are on the mat when you're cutting.

SVG Files

Scalable Vector Graphics are also known as 'SVG' files and are one of the most common file types to use for creating Cricut designs. You can import or export SVG files from Inkscape. SVG files don't rely on pixels, but rather 'vector' data to allow you to see the image (Morris, 2020). The fantastic thing about SVGs is that you can scale them to any resolution without compromising the quality of the 'image.' In our case, we can use SVG files (in Inkscape, Design Space, Photoshop, etc.) to make designs for Cricut to cut out.

Adaptive Tool System

One of the tools that can greatly enhance the capabilities of the Cricut Maker is the Maker's Adaptive Tool System. This system is only designed for the Maker model and can assist with controlling the Maker's tools (George, 2020). The Adaptive Tool System essentially uses mathematical algorithms and intricate brass gears to help make the Maker's cutting capabilities more precise.

Heat Transfer Vinyl (HTV)

When we refer to "Heat Transfer Vinyl," we're referring to the type of vinyl material that can be transferred on to project surfaces via heat transfer — i.e.. using the EasyPress to secure an iron-on vinyl to a project surface. The abbreviated version of "Heat Transfer Vinyl" is 'HTV.' In the same category (of vinyl), one of the main manufacturers of the HTV which we use for Cricut projects is Siser Easyweed, so if you come across a project that requires Siser Easyweed, they're simply referring to a brand of HTV.

Vinyl can also be differentiated by numbers such as 631, 651, or 951. The first category of vinyl is 631 Vinyl is simply 'removable' vinyl that is like a sticker. The 631 can be used for temporary wall art, window stickers, and other indoor objects that don't face a lot of external pressures such as the weather changes. There are two types of permanent vinyl, known as 651 and 951. The first Permanent Vinyl, the 651, is used for outdoor purposes and is waterproof, so it can be used to stick onto any surface that is exposed to the weather. The other vinyl category is the 951 Permanent vinyl. The 951 is marine-grade, meaning that it's stronger than the standard, permanent 651 adhesive capabilities (the higher the number, the stronger the grade of adhesiveness).

'Oracal' is one of the manufacturers of adhesive (stick-on) vinyl, such as the 631, 651, and 951 vinyl.

Thereafter, you get printable vinyl which is a sheet of vinyl that you can load into your inkjet or normal laser printer, you'll just need to ensure that the type of vinyl is the correct type for your printer. Generally speaking, printable vinyl is usually used with the "Print and Cut" function on Design Space.

The Weeding Tool

One of the more common terms that you'll come across when Cricutting is to 'weed' or to use your "weeding tool." The weeding tool is essentially a little pen-shaped tool with a needle-like head that you use to peel away any excess vinyl once you've cut your design with your Cricut. The weeding tool's main purpose is to mainly assist with vinyl projects. When Cricut instructions for projects tell you to "weed away any excess vinyl," you'll need to grab your weeding tool and carefully use the tool to pull out any excess vinyl that isn't part of the design. Alternatively, you can use tweezers or your fingers, but you'll have to be careful when it comes to the smaller and more intricate cuts and designs.

Carriage

In all of the Cricut machines, there is a compartment in the body called the 'carriage' where you can store your blades and other tools and accessories. The carriage moves back and forth along roller bars, like a cupboard drawer, so as to allow you easy access to your tools.

Cricut's Dial

On your Cricut machine (except for the Maker and the Joy), you'll find a little knob or dial that's used to select the material that you're going to be working with. You simply just adjust the dial to whichever material that you're working with and if you can't find that material option on the dial, you can choose the 'Custom' option and just select the material of choice in Design Space, prior to cutting. You'll have to choose the material before cutting, as well as set up the necessary blades, mat, and material into your machine.

Digital Cartridges

In Design Space, you may also come across the term "digital cartridges." Physical cartridges were needed for the older models of Cricut machines, but the newer models have removed the need for it, so, nowadays, you're more likely to see the term "digital cartridges" in replace of physical ones. Digital cartridges are essentially images that are grouped by something similar, such as an artist. However, the term "digital cartridges" was recently replaced with the name "image sets" now on Digital Space.

The Cricut's Rollers and Roller Bars

A few of the main functions on all of the models are their rollers and roller bars. The rollers and the small rubber wheels are near the entry where you load in your mat. It helps you to easily roll the mat and material into the machine without hassle. The roller bars are the two metal bars across the width of the machine that help the carriage move back and forth.

The bars also rotate to help the Cricut cut in any direction, with ease.

Star Wheels

Cricut machines also come with Star Wheels that are little white gears that sit on the roller bars to help secure the materials to the mat. There are times when certain projects will ask you to consider shifting or adjusting the star wheels around, especially when you're cutting thicker materials with the Knife Blade.

While these are merely a few of the more common parts of your Cricut machine (and some tools for your toolkit), the range is ever-growing. The Cricut website is the best place to keep updated on the range of tools and accessories for your powerful, little machine and you can also peruse the catalog for any deals or promotions. There are hundreds of options for different styled and strengths of blades, as well as different styles and colors of pens available to build your glorious collection of Cricut accessories; thus, allowing you to continuously explore your range of project options and make the most unique end products!

Tools & Accessories for Your Cricut

In terms of understanding the physical body of your Cricut machine, we must first understand that aside from the physical body of the machine, the tools and accessories designed for each machine can exponentially enhance the capabilities and precision of the machine's cutting capabilities. For instance, understanding the types of blades and pens for different machines and materials can help the machine cut with much more efficiency and precision.

The Bonded Fabric Blade

The Bonded Fabric Blade is a blade that works with the Maker and Explore range, and it can be used to cut fabric with its blade backed with an ironed stabilizer to help stiffen it for support. The Bonded Fabric Blade comes in pink housing (the metal piece that holds the blade) and can help cut through tougher material or help with more intricate designs, due to its stabilized support system.

Types of Cricut Mats

Mats are another thing that you'll be making a lot of use of — it's required for any type of cutting to take place. The Cricut Joy is the only machine that can cut certain materials without the need for a mat. The mats are removable and have sort of an adhesive texture to it, so as to help the materials stay in place while the cutting process is happening. When you prepare your Cricut machine to cut, you'll need to load a mat into the machine along with your material of choice. Types of mats vary depending on the material that you're using (similar to the machine's blades). There are five types of mats: StandardGrip, LightGrip, FabricGrip, and the Cricut Joy Card Mat. The mats are based on the material type that you're using, what you need done (cutting, sewing, etc.) as well as the size of the design and machine. You can use your mat guide (the small, plastic guide) as a reference to help you properly insert the mat into the machine.

The Cricut Joy (the most recent addition to the Cricut family) has a considerably high amount of tools, accessories, and materials specifically designed for it. One of which is the Card Mat. The Card Mat is a mat that allows your Joy to quickly create cards by using pre-designed cards in Design Space. If you enjoy creating cards for others and you have the Joy, this can be a handy little tool to grab, to ease the card making and cutting process.

Smart Materials

The Cricut Joy doesn't only come with unique materials and tools, it can also work mat-less with some materials (unlike the rest of the Cricut range that requires a mat to cut). The Joy can work with materials known as 'Smart' materials (which are specifically created to work with the Joy), and come in forms of materials such as vinyl, infusible ink, and writable labels. The Joy can also cut much longer cuts without needing the traditional Cricut mat.

Fine Point Blade, Deep Cut Blade, and Knife Blade

The Deep Cut Blade comes in a black housing and works with the Cricut Maker and Explore machines. It's a blade designed to cut through much thicker materials such as leather and craft foam. The Fine Point Blade is a bit finer than the Deep Cut Blade, and the Cricut Maker's Knife Blade is a bit sharper. The Fine Point Blade comes in a silver or gold housing and is the standard blade in all of the Cricut machines, as it can cut through various materials such as paper, card stock, vinyl, etc. The Knife Blade is created specifically for use of the Maker and is used to cut through tougher material such as balsa wood, basswood, leather, chipboard, etc.

Perforation Blade

Another tool that's specific to the Cricut Maker is the Perforation Blade which, in its name, is self-explanatory. The Perforation Blade is simply used to help perforate lines into paper and cardstock which can greatly help with assembling pieces of a pattern together, for instance. The Rotary Blade is another tool specific to the Maker and is shaped like a small pizza cutter that can be used to glide through materials rather than dragging them when cutting. It's mainly used on tougher and thicker fabrics such as leather and felt, among other thicker fabrics.

Wavy Blade

The Wavy Blade is a tool specific to the Cricut Maker and can work with QuickSwap. It's one of the most exciting blades to add to your collection, especially if you like some funky patterns in your cuts! The Wavy Blade, as its name suggests, allows the machine to cut wavy lines into your material of choice, creating a groovy and smooth touch to your end project!

Debossing Tool

Another tool specific to the Maker is the debossing tool, and it's used to help create a gorgeous, embossed look in paper and cardstock! The tool can up your game in designing, creating, and cutting cards; if you're looking for a Cricut machine to help you create unique and custom cards, the debossed tool is a must-have in your tool kit!

Engraving Tool & Fabric Pen

Similar to the debossing tool, the Cricut Maker can also make use of the Engraving tool that can carve into surfaces such as acrylic or metal. In regards to fabrics, the Maker can also work with a tool called the Fabric Pen that works hand-in-hand with the Maker's rotary blade. The Fabric Pen can help ease the process of sewing, by creating little markings on the patterns once it's cut, so that you know where to stitch or match pieces together. Some people grab a pen holder and a few sharpies from their local store and use it in place of the Fabric Pen if they need a quick back up.

Aside from the Fabric Pen, all Cricut machines do come with a standard pen and holder, which can be instructed to write on different materials such as cards and papers. Cricut does offer a variety of pens and markers in different colors, styles, and types so that you have a plethora of options to choose from! There's also a new addition in the Maker model that allows you to easily make use of multiple tools instead of needing to constantly change the entire housing. With the Quick-Swap function, you just need to change out the tip of the tool by pressing on a plunger on the Maker, and then simply swap the tooltips! It's an amazing little addition that greatly enhances the capabilities and efficiency of the Maker.

Scoring Stylus

The Scoring Stylus is specifically used by the Maker and Explore range and is essentially a tool that creates a score in materials such as cardstock to create an easy line for folding. Similarly, the Scoring Wheel is only used by the maker and instead of only scoring the material like the Scoring Stylus, the Wheel drags across the cardstock (material) with its wheel to create a much deeper and more distinct line. The Scoring Wheel can come as a single wheel for easy scoring (for cardstock) or a double wheel for much deeper scoring on tougher, well-coated materials.

Tips on Cleaning Your Machine

Aside from all the amazing capabilities of the Cricut machines, and the possibilities that they offer, the machines are also quite easy to maintain with hassle-free cleaning.

The most you'd need to do with the machine is ensure that the mats are cleaned regularly so that they aren't worn down after a while, but other than that, there are a few handy little tricks to keep the machine spick and span, without needing to spend too much time disassembling the machine for an entire wash!

Creating a habit of cleaning the machine frequently is a great way to reduce the need to dedicate hours deep cleaning the machine, especially because the cleaning process is pretty low maintenance.

Cricut mats are the most used accessories for the Cricut machine, and because of its sticky quality (to hold the material), it can quickly gather up debris from cutting the materials and lose its adhesiveness quite quickly. If you're planning to lightly clean your mat, you can just use the plastic scraper that comes with your Cricut machine to lightly scrape any debris off of the mat. You can then go in with some baby wipes or a lint roller if there's still some residue stuck to the mat.

If you're using disposable wipes, use baby wipes or disinfectant wipes that are bleach-free and alcohol-free, so that it doesn't remove the stickiness from the mat. Once dry, you can go over the mat with a lint roller, which serves two purposes for cleaning these mats: the first reason is to simply remove any excess dust or debris from the mat, and the second reason is so that the lint roller can transfer its stickiness to the mat.

If you're planning on giving your mat a full-on clean, simply bathing the mat in a dish of soapy water for 5-10 minutes is more than enough! If there are still a few stubborn bits of debris that won't wash off, you can use a small brush or sponge to lightly scrub the surface. Thereafter, you can air-dry the mat until it's ready to be used again. Try not to dry the mat with other materials such as a towel or a paper towel, as these may leave more residue on the mat (because of its stickiness) and the entire washing process will become counter-intuitive.

If your mat has started to lose its stickiness, you can buy an adhesive spray or a repositionable adhesive which are available at retail craft stores or online shops (Lokey, n.d.). These sprays are much cheaper than having to buy an entirely new mat. A good option for an adhesive spray is the Gorilla Heavy Duty Adhesive Spray which goes for about $9 on Amazon.

You'll have to clean off the mat (any remaining debris) before coating it. You can do so by simply dusting it off or using a lint roller to remove any dust. Thereafter, use a scraper to brush over the mat. Next, coat the mat with the spray and leave it to rest for about 15-20 minutes and your mat is good as new!

Cleaning the actual machine is much, much easier. You'll first need to disconnect the machine from its power source before cleaning, then grab a soft, clean cloth and some glass cleaner spray and gently wipe over the body of the machine. If you notice any areas of grease building up (this usually happens around the carriage area), you can use an absorbing agent such as cotton, tissue, or a soft cloth to wipe around the area to remove the excess grease (How do I Clean my Explore Machine? n.d.).

If you'd like to add more grease to the mechanisms in your machine, start by turning off your machine and then move the carriage to the left. Clean the carriage area (as per the instructions above), then push the carriage to the right and clean once more. Push the carriage to the center and then squeeze small amounts of grease onto a cotton swab. Apply a small amount of grease to either side of the carriage, forming a small ¼" ring on either side of the carriage with the grease. Move the carriage all the way to the left, then all the way to the right to evenly grease the entire bar. End off by wiping off any excess grease that's left on the bar.

Chapter 2: Software & the Design Space

Cricut Design Space is Cricut's official software app and is free for Cricut owners. Essentially, the aim of the app was to combine the capabilities of the Cricut machines with the power of technology to allow Cricut owner's the ability to have access to (and create) infinite amounts of designs, patterns, projects, etc. Thus, expanding the possibilities for what one can do with their Cricut machine!

The software is now available for both Windows, Mac, Android, and iOS users, and essentially acts as a cloud for users to access designs, patterns, fonts, etc. as well as to act as a bridge between creating designs and instructing the Cricut machine on what to cut or print.

Cricut also created a membership plan for its users, called Cricut Access, where they can access much more content in terms of patterns, fonts, templates, etc. to further expand their possibilities of customizing and personalizing their projects. As we have discussed in Chapter 1, there are three membership options available to Cricutters, with different benefits at different prices, ranging from $7-10 per month.

Design Space's Interface

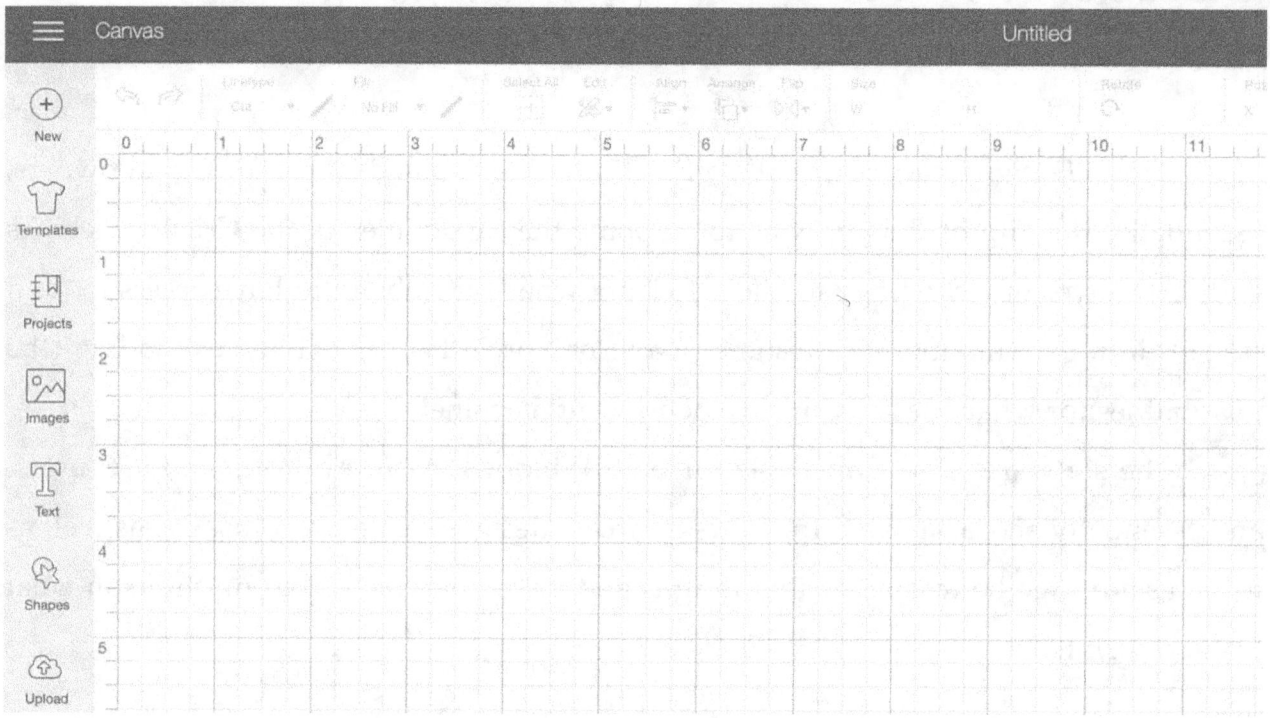

When you open up Design Space on your desktop, you'll first see a sidebar that says **"My Projects"** and if you have Cricut Access, there will also be a bottom bar that says **"Cricut Access"** (Top Tips and Tricks: the Basics of Cricut Design Space, 2017). If you continue scrolling further down the page, you'll see other project ideas from the Cricut Community. If you click on the **"View All"** you can see more projects of that similar project.

When you scroll back up to the **"My Projects"** button, you'll see a button on the left of "My Projects" that says **"New Project"** with a '**+**' sign. Alternatively, there is a green "New Project" button on the top right-hand corner. Once you click this button, you'll be redirected to a blank canvas with a grid on it.

On the top right corner of the screen, you should see your machine of choice showing up. If not, you'll need to connect your machine and choose it. Generally, with the newer Cricut models, you'll need to connect the machine via Bluetooth. Some of the older models are connected via cables.

If you'd like to change the size of your canvas' **gridlines**, you can click the corner square on the grid (next to the 0 mark). If you click the empty square once, the smaller gridlines will disappear, if you click it twice, it will make all of the gridlines disappear and if you click the square three times, the gridlines will reset to what they were in the beginning.

On the left-hand side of the window, you'll see a few functions for creating your designs: new, templates, projects, images, text, shapes, and upload. If you select '**New**,' it will just start a new project again or replace the canvas (and the work that you've done on the canvas) with a blank canvas. The '**Templates**' button will open up a page of templates to help you envision your project. The templates page will show a few suggestions of potential projects that you could create, and you can choose one of these options to help you gain a better idea of how the cut-out will work on your project surface of choice (the template). For example, if you choose the t-shirt template, you can then use this to visualize where on the t-shirt the cut-out will go. The templates are *not* cut-outs, they are simply there to help you adjust your design (for cutting) and check measurements and placements. You can either use the templates or work on the blank canvas, the two options are pretty much the same; it's just that one can help you envision the final product a bit better.

If you do choose a template to help you envision the final result and placements, you can bring it onto the canvas and adjust the measurements of the actual template to make it the exact size of the real project surface, to help you gain a better idea of the measurements for the cutout. Alternatively, you can measure the actual project surface on the physical object (such as measuring the project surface on the t-shirt that you'd like to add vinyl to) and then just create a cut-out design using those measurements.

Below 'Templates' on the left sidebar, there is a '**Projects'** function that will open up Cricut Access' Ready to Make projects. You can scroll through the projects for inspiration or simply import a project into your canvas and adjust the measurements as well as customize the design to your liking. You'll also find a large number of images (as well as SVGs) and different font options for you to bring into your canvas and customize your design!

In Cricut Access, there's also a drop-down menu where you can search for specific projects, images, or fonts to your preference. Cricut Access also categorizes its projects quite well, so you can find a bunch of ideas that are perfectly suited to your taste. There is also a category called 'Free' which you can make great use of when first learning to use your machine! The categories button is found on the left of the "Search Projects" bar, on the top right corner of Cricut Access.

Underneath the 'Projects' on the left-hand sidebar, the next button is the '**Images'** button. Naturally, this button is used to insert images from your Cricut library. There are over 100 000 images to choose from (or import your own SVG). There's a search bar at the top of the images window and you can choose from a variety of options. On the left-hand side of the images window, there's an option to filter your choices to be more precise. For instance, if you're looking for balloons, you can search for balloons in images, then filter the project type to just show options for cards with balloons images. The filters are broken down into: Cricut Access (which only shows you images from Cricut Access), project type (such as cards), operation type, image complexity, layers, ownership, brand, material, and language. If you aren't with Cricut Access, then you can filter the images under 'Ownership' to only show 'Free' images.

Once you've found an image, simply insert it into the canvas. You can do this with multiple images too by selecting a few which you like, and these images will be highlighted green. Once ready, click 'Inset' and it will be added to the canvas.

Once you've inserted an image or design onto the canvas, there will be a little bar at the top of the window that says '**Linetype**,' and the types of linetypes vary with the different Cricut machines. For instance, the Maker has the most tools and accessories, so it has the most linetypes—which is eight types: cut, draw, score, engrave, deboss, wave, perforate and foil. You will also need to load your machine's blade or pen with respect to the linetype that you chose.

If you choose '**Cut**,' this option is available with the Maker, Explore Air 2, and Joy, and you'll usually need a fine tip blade for this option. You can also choose "**Deep Cut**" which is available with the Maker and Explore Air, or the **"Knife Blade"** or **"Rotary Blade"** which are available with the Maker. The Explore Air 2 only has four linetypes—cut, draw, score, and foil; while the Joy only has two linetypes—cut and draw.

For the '**Draw**' type, you'll need to use the Pens and are available with the Joy, Explore Air 2, and Maker. 'Score' will require the scoring stylus (which is available with the Explore Air 2 and the Maker) or the scoring wheel which is available with the Maker. 'Engraving' requires the engraving tip, 'Deboss' requires the debossing tip, 'Wave' requires the wavy blade and 'Perf' requires the perforation blade—all of these four linetypes are only available with the Maker. Lastly, '**Foil**' requires the foil transfer kit which needs to be purchased separately and works with the Maker and Explore Air 2.

The option next to the linetype is the color options if you've chosen a linetype such as '**Draw**.' You can also change the pen type in the drop-down menu by the pen — the thickness of the image's lines will change depending on the type of pen you choose.

If you'd like to choose the '**Print**' option, you'll need to click on the '**Fill**' drop-down menu then choose the 'Print' option.

To change the color of the image or fill it with a pattern, click on the small box to the right of the 'Fill' button, then choose your color or pattern. If you choose a pattern, you can click on **"Edit Pattern"** on the bottom left of the **"Print type — Pattern"** drop-down. You'll then see a window of options to edit the pattern. One of the options is to scale the pattern, which you can adjust by altering the scale number or sliding the little circle left or right.

A handy little trick that Cricut machines can do is assign different cuts to different mats via the color of that mat. For instance, if you want to cut two squares, but one needs to be pink and the other needs to be white, you can change the material color for the image by selecting different colors in the menu. When the machine is cutting the shapes, it'll assign one color to each mat that you insert. If you want all of the shapes or designs to be the same color, just ensure that the image color is the same throughout.

You'll also notice the sidebar on the right of the window will start to show the layers and actions that you did to the design in the 'Layers' tab. If you'd like to alter or delete certain actions, you can click on the different tabs under 'Layers' to make those adjustments. You can also click the little eye button on the right of each action to view or hide different aspects of the design to see what looks best, or to simply focus on different sections of the design, one at a time.

Once you insert a shape or design, you can click on the **lock button** on the bottom left corner which will lock the shape in place if you're happy with the design. Similarly, you can unlock the design by clicking the button again, which can then allow you to freely resize the image and adjust as you please. You can also simply just change the measurements in the above menu if you'd like to have precise measurements.

The next function on the left-hand sidebar is the '**Text**' button, which is below 'Images.' Creating texts is quite easy if you've dealt with Word, Pages, Powerpoint, or Keynote as the design process is quite similar. Simply select the 'Text' button and a text box will pop up on the screen. Type in your desired word or phrase into the text box and adjust to your preferences. You can use the functions in the above menu to adjust font, size, color, style, etc. If you choose a multi-layer font (fonts with shadows), the shadow is usually hidden whilst you type. You can click on the little eye button next to the text's layer, on the right-hand sidebar to view the shadow.

If you want to edit an individual letter in the text, simply click on the text (on the canvas) and then click on the '**Ungroup**' button on the right-hand corner. Once the letters are individualized, you can adjust them as you please, then when you're done, select the text again and group the text together.

Below the 'Text' function, there's the '**Shapes**' tool. This opens up a few of the basic shape options, similar to what you'd find on a Word or Pages document.

The last button on the left-hand sidebar is the '**Upload**' button. This function allows you to upload your images and designs into the canvas. Design Space can only work with files that are .jpg, .gif, .png, .bmp, .svg or .dxf. If you need to change the format of your file, you can do so in apps such as Photoshop. If you purchase files online though, you can also check if these file options are possible. *Etsy*, for example, offers the option for the .svg format which can greatly help keep the quality of the image intact, regardless of how you'd like to resize and alter the design.

If you upload a pattern, the pattern will appear next to the 'Fill' menu, under **"Print Type."**

Naturally, you'll need to try to use the highest quality images possible because if you use lower quality images, the cut will only be as good as that—which is why .svg images are usually the best option for Design Space.

When your image is uploaded into the software, you can edit it as you'd like by re-sizing, adjusting, etc. Design Space does have a few tools that are similar to Photoshop, such as the Wand, Eraser, and Crop tools, so if you're familiar with photo editing programs, you'll be able to easily maneuver your way around this stage. Essentially, the 'Want' tool can be used to remove an entire color of an area that you select (for example, a background), while the eraser tool is used to manually erase areas of an image.

Once you're done with your design, you can then **save the image** and be presented with two options: either saving the image as a print then cutting or saving the design as a cut image. It's always best to save the design as the first option (save image as print then cut) because then you'll be able to have the option of printing or cutting the image when you'd like to, whereas the "saving the design as a cut image" will only allow you to cut the design in the future.

Moving onto the right-hand sidebar, also known as the 'Layers' menu, you'll be faced with a few functions such as slice, weld, attach, flatten and contour. '**Slice**' is used when you want to split overlapping layers into separate parts so that you can work on them individually. '**Weld**' is used to combine multiple layers into one part. '**Attach**' is used to hold images in a position for cutting. '**Flatten**' is used to merge the layers into one printable image and '**Contour**' is used to hide or show the lines on a layer. In addition to this, the 'Layers' menu will also show all the images and texts on your canvas, and if you click on them, you can see the adjustments made. You can also see the top bar menu change when you click on a layer, which offers you more options to alter the image.

At the *bottom* right-hand corner, you'll see a few buttons on the 'Layers' tab. The first button says '**Slice**,' this will help you to slice two overlapping layers (it can only do two layers at a time). In doing so, you will then see three layers on your layer's tab, from the image. Thereafter, you can delete any unwanted layers by right-clicking on the layer in the layer's tab and selecting 'Delete.'

Next to the 'Slice' tool is the '**Weld**' tool, which helps join images and texts together to create one single design. It's important to note that welding images together is a permanent action, so you cannot un-weld the design at a later point. If you want to weld the design, but you're worried that you may need to unweld it at a later stage, you can duplicate the design and then click the little eye button on the duplicated layer (so that it's hidden), and then weld the one that's visible. If you find that you won't need the un-welded image at a later stage, you can go ahead and delete it.

On the right of the 'Weld' tool is the '**Attach**' tool. The attach tool can fasten an image in place so when you cut the image, it cuts exactly as you'd arranged it in the canvas. For instance, if you made a star shape by arranging triangles, the Cricut will cut the design in that arrangement. If the design wasn't attached, then the Cricut will just cut a bunch of triangles in a nonspecific manner, and you'll have to manually assemble the triangles to make a star shape. The attach tool can also be used to write or score lines onto a cut layer.

The second-last tool is the '**Flatten**' tool, and this is used with the "print then cut" feature, as it takes multi-layered images and flattens them into a single image— similar to welding, but it can take numerous layers and it only works with the "cut then print" function. For instance, if you want your Cricut to cut a design and print something onto that cut, you can use this function. Additionally, you can also 'Unflatten' this image whenever you'd like, which will turn it back into multiple layers.

Lastly, the '**Contour**' tool is used to remove unwanted pieces of an image and can only work with cut images and one layer and a time. For instance, if there are negative spaces within a cut image that you don't want the Cricut machine to cut, you can use the contour tool to delete those negative spaces.

You can do this by clicking on the pieces directly in the image and removing them with the contour tool, or delete them from the right-hand side menu (in the contour tool window). In the contour tool window, you'll also notice that the image will appear in a light-grey color, but when there are pieces of the image that have been deleted, those areas will turn a darker grey.

Next to the 'Layer' tab is the **"Color Sync"** tab. If you click on that, you can drag and drop different layers to make them the same color—which comes in handy if you're choosing multiple images and fonts and want to make it all the same color. It'll also help the cutting process as the Cricut will detect that the designs are all the same color and will cut it all at the same time.

When you're ready to make your project, you can click the green button at the top right-hand corner that says **"Make It."** You'll then be redirected to a preview screen of the mat. If you click on the three dots, you can move your image to another mat or hide it (if there's a specific image out of multiple images that you don't want to cut), by selecting the image and then selecting the '**Hide**' option. You can also rotate your image.

On the top left-hand side of the window, you can see an option for **"Project Copies"** where you can adjust the number of copies you'd like to print or cut; it will then be adjusted on your mat to show you how many cuts you can do per mat.

There's also an option to change your **mat size**, in the left-hand sidebar. Once you're ready and happy with your image to cut or print, simply click the green 'Continue' button on the bottom right corner and load up your Cricut machine with the necessary materials and tools! Design space will also instruct you on what to do, if the machine needs to be re-loaded, or if something hasn't been loaded properly.

Troubleshooting

One of the biggest things that you'll just need to consider when working in Design Space is which functions are permanent and which functions are not. For instance, the 'Weld' tool can't be changed once it has been added, so you'll need to start from scratch again.

Other than that, most of the functions on Design Space are quite easy to troubleshoot or alter, if you come across any issues. For instance, if you've lost data on a font or image that you've used, and you'd like to record it for future purposes, you can simply right click on the font or image in the layer's tab, then scroll to the bottom of the drop-down menu. At the bottom of the menu, there should be an option that says **"Image Info."** If you click on that, it will tell you the image's number. If you search for that number in Design Space, it will direct you to the image in image search. Similarly, you can use this on fonts. If you manipulate the font or weld it, the name might disappear from the Layers menu, so you can follow the same process of right-clicking on the font to see the "Image Info," and the information on your font will be there.

Another important tip before cutting images or texts is to make sure that you've mirrored the design before proceeding so that the cut faces the same way as you read it in Design Space.

If you're using Invisible Ink Patterns and you'd like to see a preview of the design before cutting, you can go onto the Cricut website and look for the Infusible Ink pattern that you're using. Click on the swatch and grab a screenshot of the pattern (as maximized as possible). Next, upload the screenshot into Design Space and select the "Pattern Fill" option (note that you may have to change the file format of the screenshot, which you can easily do by renaming the end of the file in .jpg or .png if Design Space shows an error message that it cannot work with the screenshot). To make things a bit easier for yourself, you can also name the pattern after its name on Cricut's website.

Once you have your image of choice on your canvas, you can change the image to a print image in the 'Fill' option, in the above menu. Next, select the 'Pattern' option, next to 'Fill' and you should see your pattern's swatch there.

If you encounter any software-related issues, it's always good to try two options before exploring further: rebooting or reconnecting to your wifi and restarting the software. Generally speaking, wifi connection can be a tumultuous thing to deal with, so checking your connectivity and strength of the connection may just help relieve some of the issues that you might be facing with Design Space (Tips for Solving Cricut Design Space Problems, 2020). Inconsistent wifi connection or dips and spikes of connectivity can cause your software to start bugging out or crash. Try to check your speed before starting your program (which you can do by simply Googling "wifi test" to check your upload and download speeds). Try to also work as close to your wifi router as possible, if you have a slower or unstable connection so that you can get as much strength from the connection as possible. If you are experiencing slower wifi connectivity, try to close any other sites that you may be using (such as Youtube, or a music streaming platform) so that your wifi connection can strengthen. If this still doesn't work, you can try to reboot your wifi modem.

Cricut's Design Space works best with a minimum of 2-3 Mbps download speed, and a minimum of 1 Mbps of uploading speed. If you are running a test to check your wifi connection's strength, try to ensure that these are the lowest connection speeds so that your software can run smoothly.

Additionally, although the software can run on most devices, it does require a few basic elements from the device to run efficiently. For Windows computers, Design Space requires:

- Windows 8 or later to run efficiently

- Intel Core series or an AMD processor

- at least 4GB of Ram

- at least 50MB of free disk space

- a USB port or Bluetooth connection (which works with the newer Cricut models).

For Apple computers, Design Space requires:

- Mac OS X 10.12 or anything more recent

- CPU of at least 1.83 GHz

- at least 4GB of Ram

- at least 50MB of free space

- a USB port or Bluetooth connection

If your wifi connection is still okay *and* your computer is running fine, then you may want to also look into whether there's interference with other programs that may be running in the background. Try to close any background programs as this may just be weirdly interfering with Design Space's ability to run optimally.

You can also try to clear your internet's cache and history, check up on your anti-virus software and run an update if necessary, try updating drivers (if you're using Windows), defragment your hard drive or run a malware check. These are all issues that may just be slowing down your computer's speed and ability to run Design Space optimally.

Alternatively, you could try to use a different browser for Design Space—for instance, if you're using Safari, try to see if other browsers such as Chrome or Firefox work with the software. Design Space can work with all browsers, but sometimes specific browsers suddenly struggle to load specific websites, so you might be able to run the software more efficiently on another browser. Also ensure that your browser is up to date, as that could also be a possible issue.

If you have tried everything and you're still struggling to find the root cause, Cricut does have a call center that you can access from their website. Alternatively, you can also try to Google the issue to see if others have experienced a similar issue. The Cricut online community is quite large and there should be some blog posts or Youtube videos online to help you with any Cricut-related issues.

Alternative Software & Apps

The Cricut community is large, and thanks to social media and the internet, the community has grown in numbers, strength, and project ideas! Due to the ever-growing popularity of the range, the options for projects, templates, curated image packs, designs, and images by fellow Cricutters have grown.

Some of the more renowned Cricut bloggers have put together packages of their favorite images, designs, and project ideas for their audiences to follow along. If you don't have Cricut Access and you do have certain Cricut bloggers that you follow, you can always check to see if they have any curated packs on their website which you can just download and try out. This is also a great way for beginners to dip their toes in the water before fully diving into the Cricut world. It also offers you the ability to chat with others within the community (or the blogger) if you need help on a specific project.

A lot of programs can work hand-in-hand with Design Space primarily because of the files that it can handle (such as vector files—which are the .svg files). If you're designing an image or would like to alter an image before bringing it into Design Space, you can use programs such as Adobe Photoshop or Adobe Illustrator to help you alter the design and export in a file that's compatible with Design Space. However, there are other programs similar to Photoshop or Illustrator that are online or on the app store for download. Bloggers such as Jennifer Maker (Maker, n.d.), The Happy Scraps (The Happy Scraps, n.d.), and The Girl Creative (The Girl Creative, n.d.) are a few fantastic blogs to consider checking out if you'd like some gorgeous project ideas or a few free images and designs! The Girl Creative, for instance, has downloadable free cut files and free printables on her website.

If Design Space is down or you're simply looking for some variety of software options, here are some with similar features: Sure Cuts a Lot, Make the Cut, Inkscape, and Silhouette Studio (Robert, n.d.).

Sure Cuts

Sure Cuts a Lot is quite a popular alternative for Design Space because it works extremely well with Cricut machines and designs. The software offers you the option of creating designs with the standard layout—offering tools for drawing, designing, coloring, editing, resizing, and adding texts. Sure Cuts a Lot is not only highly compatible with Cricuts machines, but it's also compatible with a lot more plugins. Therefore, if you are looking to create more unique and custom designs, Sure Cuts a Lot can help you expand your options of tools and materials in this area (due to the expansive array of plug-ins available). The software also updates automatically and offers you full control of designs. The only issue with the program is that some features aren't compatible with certain Macs, and the software can only tackle one project at a time, so it might not be the best suited for you if you need a high production demand.

Make the Cut

Make the Cut is a third-party software that you can use for die-cutting designs and has most of the functions that Design Space offers. Like Sure Cuts a Lot, Make the Cut has a high compatibility rate and is also extremely reliable (as it's been on the market for quite a while). Make the Cut is also great for editing as it has more advanced tools and features for tracing and editing images. One of the only issues is that the software isn't compatible with Cricut machines, so you'll have to use it like Photoshop or Illustrator, just to edit images then bring them into a software such as Sure Cuts a Lot or Design Space to connect to the Cricut machine. In addition to this, Make the Cut is also reportedly faulty with Macs. On the plus side, if you're looking for fast and reliable software, with a greater abundance of editing features for designs, Make the Cut can offer that much.

Inkscape

Inkscape is another considerably popular software used by Cricutters. What makes it so popular is that it's a free program that offers the best of features—in contrast to the two aforementioned programs. Inkscape allows you to do it all: draw, layer, manipulate images, import and export files with the best of quality. You can also create .svg files with ease and the editing tools offered by Inkscape can be especially helpful to boost the power of editing images and designs. If you love to design images or edit images, Inkscape will excite the editor in you! Beginners who are looking to broaden their horizons in terms of editing images can also benefit from Inkscape because it has so many features and tools, *and* it's free. In addition to this, Inkscape is completely compatible with Linux, Windows, and macOS and works with almost all design file formats. The only downside is that the interface may be a little complex to use at first, but it's a fantastic learning tool to better your editing skills if anything!

Silhouette Studio

Silhouette Studio shines its brightest for those who are interested in textile designing and embroidering rather than die-cutting; although, the software works similarly to the aforementioned software. Silhouette Studios is a fantastic option for editing images as it offers an array of powerful editing tools and is compatible with most file formats. It's also compatible with Cricut machines and can also merge well with other editing programs. The only downfalls of Silhouette Studio are that you may have to pay for some features and the installing process might be a bit tricky — but once you're in, it's pretty similar (in terms of its interface) to other design apps!

Judging by the few aforementioned design apps, finding an alternative for Design Space isn't that tough of a task to tackle. However, it'd be best to familiarize yourself with the general editing tools and interface (such as the canvas, layers, etc.) so that no matter which program you decide to use, you'll be able to maneuver through it with ease and thus, be able to reap more from what the software has to offer.

Chapter 3: Materials & Techniques

The true power of Cricut comes in its ability to powerfully evolve in terms of capabilities. From where Cricut has started to now, the machines are able to not only tackle paper and tissue paper but now handle a wide variety of materials such as leather, fabric, cake decorating materials, vinyl, foam, etc. In addition to this, Cricuts have also expanded their range of material tools and accessories to handle these types of materials.

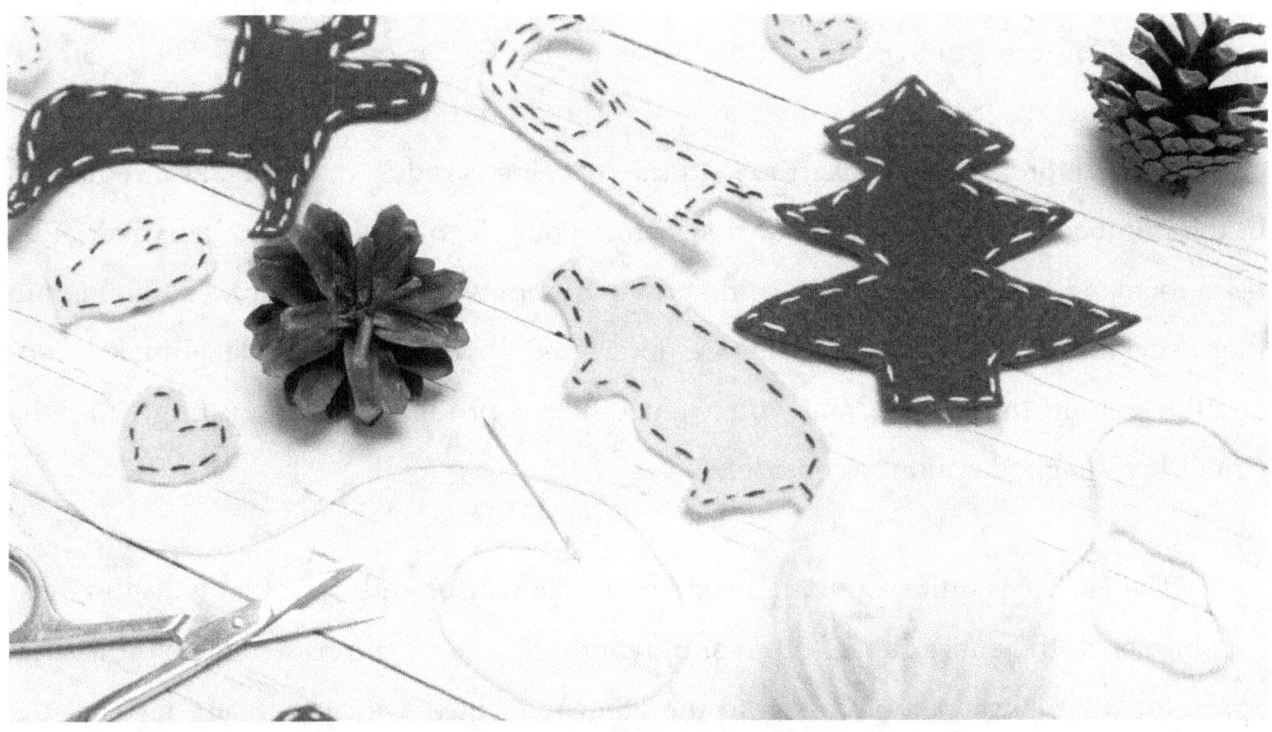

We have also just uncovered how expansive Design Space is in terms of exploring different design options and project types. The range of machines and their accessories do shine brightest with specific materials and projects, and we aim to explore that in this chapter. We aim to see which machines work best with what materials, and how you can efficiently use your machine to gain the highest quality end product, with the quickest production time.

For instance, if we look at the Cricut Joy model, it shines its brightest when dealing with larger quantities of card-making or label-making projects. Because the Joy is so small and compact, it's been made to specifically perform best with certain materials and project types (such as the cards and labels). In addition to this, the Joy is unique in the sense that it can load much longer rolls of material (of up to 20 feet), so if you're looking for a machine that can tackle cutting a large number of small cuts in one go, the Joy is a fantastic option.

In addition to this, the Joy has an exclusive range of materials, known as 'Smart' materials. You can purchase Smart materials on the Cricut online store. These 'Smart' materials (such as 'Smart' iron-on vinyl) don't require the machine to have a mat for cutting. Therefore, the time taken to load the machine is reduced, as well as a reduction in the number of resources needed. It also cuts your cleaning time in half, as you often need to spend time cleaning mats and spraying them with adhesive sprays to maintain their stickiness. In essence, if you are interested in card-making, label-making, or anything along those lines, and you want efficient production and cutting time, the Cricut Joy is a good option to consider.

The Maker is quite a unique machine. It's powerful and versatile, with the most capabilities in the entire range. From simply judging the functions available on Design Space for the Maker in comparison to the other machines, we can already tell that the Maker is the go-to machine to get the most versatility for handling materials and projects. The Maker can print, sew, cut, deboss, and emboss. It has the most tools and accessories available, and thus, has the greatest capabilities and range out of all of the Cricut machines. The only downside with the Maker is that it's a bit on the pricier side, but if it does fit in your budget and you are looking for a long-term machine that can tackle various materials and project types, the Maker is your go-to.

The Explore Air 2 sits comfortably in the middle of the Maker and the Joy. It can handle all of the materials that the Joy can tackle, and most of the materials and functions which the Maker can do. If you're looking for a versatile middle-man machine, the Explore Air 2 is a pretty handy machine to consider. The Explore Air 2 only has four tools for cutting, writing, and scoring so if you're looking for a machine more specified towards cutting and scoring, the Explore Air 2 can be a great option, but if you want to explore other functions of Cricut machines such as sewing or dealing more with fabrics, then you may want to look into the Maker.

When we consider what materials Cricut machines can handle, they truly can take on a wide variety of over 100 materials. Some of the categories which Cricuts can tackle can be broken up into the following categories: paper and cardstock, vinyl (which is extremely popular), iron-ons, fabrics and textiles, foils, wood, and stencils for etching or debossing. Not to mention the Martha Stewart Range which can tackle cake decorating materials such as fondants.

All models work extremely well the basic materials such as vinyl, iron-on materials, and paper or cardstock, as these were the basis for where Cricut machines had started. So if you are looking for a machine to tackle these sorts of materials, any Cricut model will work well! However, if you are looking to mass-produce (small-sized) products, then you may want to look into the Joy as its writing and cutting speed is the fastest out of all of the models; and, because it can load up to 20 feet worth of material, the Joy can cut a large number of designs at once. Additionally, Joy's specific Smart range can also help speed up the cutting process.

Now that we've come to understand where each machine shines its brightest, we can then choose a machine that's best suited for our needs. On top of that, we can now work towards exploring more neat and handy little tricks on how to further enhance our machine's efficiency and get the most out of our machine!

Making the Most Out of Your Machine

One of the most important tips in relation to handling delicate cut-outs is: when working with the mat, try to peel the mat away from the cut-out design rather than the opposite way. In doing so, you're protecting the cut-out from the risk of being distorted when you tug against it. **Cut-outs** can be quite tricky to handle and can easily be distorted if not handled properly, and this could risk you losing material and time in the process. That's why tools (such as the weeding tool) and tips (such as the one aforementioned) exist, to help handle such delicate materials.

Making use of tools on Design Space (such as the Weld, Contour, and Slice tool) can greatly help you take an image or design from the cloud and easily customize it to your liking, in less time and effort than creating something from scratch. Try to explore these tools and grow your skillset in relation to handling these tools, as they can help you in creating unique designs with ease! The weld, contour, and slice tools are found at the bottom right-hand side of Design Space's interface. On the off-chance that you aren't able to choose these tools, it may be because the design or image that you've chosen isn't compatible with those tools. However, this is highly unlikely.

Similarly, the **color sync tool** (the tab to the right of the 'Layers' menu, on the right-hand side of the window) can also be of great use in choosing colors and making them similar to other shades within that color. In doing so, you can easily set a standard color in an image and ease the printing or drawing process for your Cricut (20 Cricut Design Space Tips & Tricks You'll Really Want to Know, 2019). For instance, if you have an image of a pineapple on your canvas, and the fruit is mixed with shades of yellow and brown, you can choose the color sync tool and make the entire pineapple one standard shade of yellow. Although this does make the image flatter, it does help with printing designs for signs or cards, etc. with less time and resources needed.

You can also use the color sync tool to make elements of one design the same as another design on the canvas so that your Cricut can print or cut those images together to save on time and resources. An example of this is if you had a blue beach ball and a red heart on your canvas, you can make both of the images the same color to help speed up the process of cutting or printing and reduce the number of resources used. You can also use this tool if you want the designs to match a specific color theme.

Another little trick to help speed up your process in Design Space is to experiment with your search results to see how you can easily access the most results, specific to your search. Design Space's **search function** is extremely sensitive, so try to explore the search options in your spare time to see what your general search categories would be like and you can 'Favorite' some images and designs and categorize them for later use. You can also jot down search words that show the most results, or a few of your favorite search results so that you can refer to these notes whenever you need to quickly look for specific designs or images.

You can also experiment with the search results by trying different synonyms (or words related to the search word) for the search word, to see if there are any other results that could work with your design's theme. For instance, if you're searching for a 'Circle' you can also search for 'Round' to look for more options. If you're searching for Valentine's themed designs, you can also search for 'Hearts,' 'Love,' or 'Cupid' for more options. Because the search results are so sensitive, Design Space's results might only show results for one specific word – ie. if you're searching for Valentine's day results, it might not show you results for 'Cupid' or other images that could pertain to that theme.

The results are so specific that the results can vary by the difference of a single letter, for instance, you might find that results for 'Hearts' are different from the results for 'Heart.' You can try to play around with the search word if you'd like to see more options.

Similarly, if you'd like to only scroll through free designs and images, make use of the filters in the search results section. There's an option in 'Filter' next to the search bar, which you can simply adjust to only search for free images and designs. You can also make use of the filter option to only show designs for specific projects, materials, etc. You can also filter the font search results to only show free options.

To promote greater efficiency, you can also look into **shortcuts** on your keyboard. If you scroll through your menus, you'll find the shortcuts next to each function (for instance, if you want to copy something, it'll show the control button + 'C'). Learning these shortcuts can help quicken the pace of working so that you don't have to maneuver through the interface every time you need to perform a function.

In addition to this, if you're using Design Space, you may notice that the crop tool is missing. If you'd like to crop an image or design, and you're working with Design Space, you can use the slice tool in conjunction with the free shapes (such as a square shape) to crop your design.

Once you're ready with your design and head on over to the preview window, you can **rearrange** the designs on the mats so that you can make the most out of the material used. For instance, Design Space may have dedicated four designs to each mat, but you want to cut six designs and the software then requires you to have two mats (four designs on one mat, and two on another mat). You can simply rearrange the positions of the designs on the mat to fit the other two designs in, so you can use one mat and sheet of material, rather than wasting a second mat and sheet of material! To rearrange the designs, all you have to do is simply click on one of the designs and you can drag it around the mat. When the design is selected, two or three little dots on the corners of the image will appear which can help you rotate the image, etc. to help fit more designs on the mat or create as little material wastage as possible. The dot on the upper left-hand corner of the image (when selected) offers you the option of moving the image to another mat.

If you're running a few cuts at a time that requires a few mats, Design Space also offers the option of **skipping** or **repeating** a mat when you're in the cutting phase. Usually, once you've hit the "Make It" button, you just have to load your materials (with the right color and paper size) into the machine, and you're good to go! However, if you'd like to skip a mat and adjust your production process, or even repeat a mat (which is especially helpful if you need to re-cut something) you can do so with ease!

Prior to loading the mat and material into your machine, select which mat will be cut next by clicking the mat on the left-hand side so that it's highlighted, and the machine will automatically jump to that mat next. You can also click on a mat that's already been cut, to re-cut it. You will just need to ensure that when you are loading the mat and materials into the machine, and that the colors match too.

Another fancy trick that can come in handy if you're mass-producing designs or need to speed up the cutting process, is to connect **multiple machines** to the Design Space. Obviously, this will require multiple Cricut machines, but if you do have the resources, you can connect them all to Design Space via Bluetooth, USB, or both. Prior to cutting the designs, there will be an option for you to choose which machine cuts which designs. You'll just need to ensure that the right materials, mats, and tools are loaded into the correct assigned machines.

When you're cutting a design for a specific material, you can also adjust the cut settings to the specific material that you're using. When you open up the cut preview screen, you'll see the '**Materials**' option (if you're using a machine other than the Maker, you'll have to adjust the dial on the physical machine to the material option as well). Click on "Browse all Materials," then click on "Material Settings" at the bottom of the window. You can then choose your material of choice and adjust any other settings for cutting your material (such as the depth of the cutting passes and how many passes the machine should make).

Projects such as iron-on projects (especially designs with texts) need to be reversed prior to cutting so that it's legible when cut. This step should be considered a basic and necessary step prior to cutting—it's just as important as loading the right mat and materials into your machine. You can easily achieve this step when you're on the cut preview window. There should be a function that says 'Mirror' below each mat on the left-hand sidebar. Turn the mirror function on, and it should automatically flip your design on your main design preview.

When loading your machine, Design Space does take you through easy-to-understand step-by-step processes and little reminders on how to properly load your machine, to ensure that the machine has the correct materials for the cut. From designing and creating your cuts, all the way through to loading your machine, these handy little tips can have you smooth-sailing your way through the design process!

Tips for Your Machine

Now that we have covered a few handy techniques to help the production process of your Cricut projects; here are a few last additional points to consider for dealing with whichever Cricut model you're working with (Bellis, 2020).

The Cricut Joy is the best for smaller projects, everyday use, and the best for making cards and labels. You don't have to worry much about using mats with the Joy because of its use of Smart Materials (which can save you time and money). The Joy can also work with over 50 material types. You can also use the Insert Card mat (that's pre-scored) with the Cricut card packs to cut paper-cut cards up to 4.5x6.25"—which can save you more time and effort!

Due to its easy-to-use features and reduced need for additional resources, the Joy is a fantastic starting machine for Cricut beginners (and it's the cheapest out of the range). A few pointers to consider, however, is that the machine is the lowest powered machine in the range and tackles the least amount of materials out of the entire range of Cricut models, so if you do want to expand and explore other projects with other materials, this won't be possible with the Joy. If you *are* interested in just specifically using the Joy to help with cards, small vinyls, and labels, then this is perfect for you!

As the Joy is the most compact model, its designs are restricted to a maximum width of 4.5". The Joy also has tools and accessories specific to its model, so you won't be able to swap tools with the Maker and Explore Air 2. The Joy only has one clamp, so you'll need to remember to swap tools if you want to draw and cut on the same design.

The Explore Air 2 is the best machine for much larger projects and is amazing for mass-producing designs on larger projects (such as t-shirts). It can also tackle materials of up to 0.08" in thickness, so it can work well with materials such as cork or thicker boards. The Explore Air 2 can handle over 100 material types.

Since the machine is fantastic at tackling larger areas, your range of projects can expand. For instance, you can look into making wall-art or windowpane designs. In addition to this, you can do multiple functions on one design at a time as the machine has two clamps; so if you'd like to cut and draw on a design, you can do so.

The only issues that you may want to consider with the Explore Air 2 are that it can be a bit noisy on the "Fast Cut" mode and struggles to cut more delicate materials such as tissue paper (especially with regards to more intricate designs). It's also quite similar to the Maker, but the Maker offers much, much more. If you have the option to get the Maker, it may be a better investment in terms of its versatility with materials and tools.

Cricut Maker is the most popular and most sought-after model from the Cricut range, due to its amazing performance and expansive range of materials that it can tackle. The Maker is essentially the best option for pro-level DIY projects and if you'd like to explore a versatile range of materials with your Cricut machine. The Maker also pushes you to continuously grow and expand your skillset *because* of how versatile and powerful a machine it is.

The Maker can handle materials of 1" in thickness and can apply up to an astounding 9 pounds of force when cutting! In terms of functions, the Maker offers much more functions than the Explore Air 2 and Joy combined (as we've come to understand when exploring the Maker's functions in Design Space). There are also some funky blades for the Maker, such as the rotary blade, which cuts vertically and can tackle more delicate papers. There is also a wavy blade to create gorgeous wavy shapes in your materials—this, among many other tools, accessories, and functions for the Maker is why the machine shines brightest in its range.

The only thing to consider with the Maker is that because of its expansive compatibility with materials and project ideas, there's an abundance of tools and accessories for the machine that you will have to purchase. For instance, if you'd like to engrave with the Maker, you'll need to purchase the engraving tool for the Maker, as the machine only comes with basic tools. The Maker also requires a larger working space as it's such a powerful machine that's both large in size *and* heavier, so you will need to clear out an area specifically for the machine if you're planning on getting one.

One of the best parts about the Maker? It can handle over 300 types of material! If you're looking for a powerful arts and crafts companion with amazing capabilities (not to mention being a worthwhile investment), the Maker is the best buy to build your Cricut collection!

Chapter 4: Cricut Maker = Money Maker?

Once we've come to understand how to get the *most* out of whichever model you chose, we can now move on to exploring how to turn that purchase into an investment!

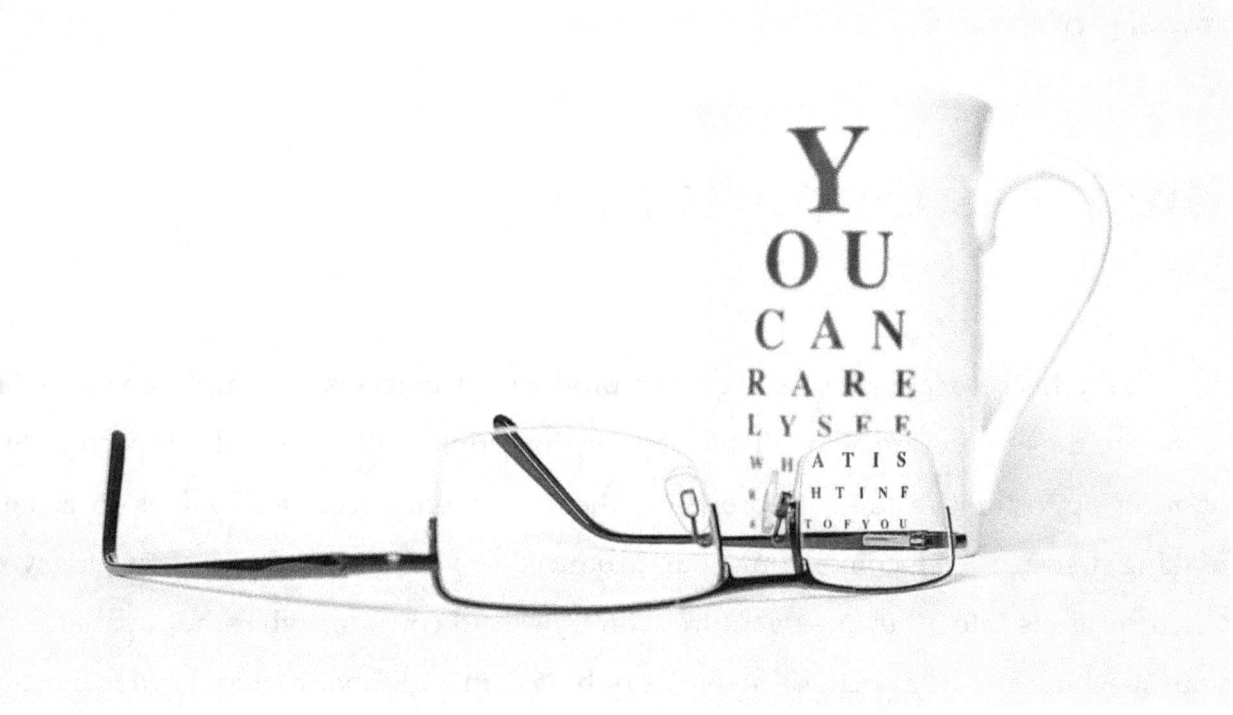

Although Cricut machines are fantastic at assisting us with all of our arts and crafts needs, it's also an amazing tool to help create the most gorgeous, personalized gifts, and act as a second source of income, by selling your end products! Considering all that the economy has been through in the past year (2020, with the pandemic), many of us are forced to stay at home as much as possible, and in turn, we have much more free time to get creative. With online stores such as Etsy and Patreon which artists can use to sell their artwork and be commissioned to create artwork, in combination with all this added free time, what's stopping us from starting up a little side-hustle?

Even if we only manage to sell a product or two a month, it's still a great source of income! In addition to this, the Cricut online community is so large that there is support and guidance from fellow Cricutters on how to optimally transform your Cricut projects into sellable products!

So, not only can you use your Cricut machine to explore your creative side, but you can also make use of the machine on creating gorgeous gifts for others, and if anything, create a business with your little machine!

Business Opportunities

Whether you plan on selling your products at markets or simply on an online platform, the options are all available at your fingertips. With online shops such as Etsy offering opportunities for entrepreneurs, there's a plethora of possibilities to achieve making a stream of income from your products! If you are thinking of turning your Cricut projects into a business venture, you'll need to consider what the capabilities of your machine are, what materials you work best with and what materials your machine works best with, and most importantly, what your brand is.

Deciding on your brand is considerably the most important factor in starting a business, because this is the foundation of your business, and this is how your market will also associate your business and its products. For instance, if you think of a fast-food restaurant, you'd think of McDonald's or Burger King. Similarly, you'll want your market to think of the products you offer (such as personalized candles that have vinyl quotes on them) and instantly think of your business. So, the first and most important thing that you'll need to determine is *what* you're selling and with what materials. You can also try to experiment with styles and aesthetics for your product to make it more unique to you and your brand. For instance, if you think of red and yellow or the yellow 'M,' your brain connects this with McDonald's. You can also explore different little tokens or Easter eggs in your products that add a little signature touch to your brand.

A few of the most profitable ways that some are making money with their Cricut machines right now are with vinyl projects, as they're easy to cut as well as easy to customize to yours or the client's desires (9 Most Profitable Cricut Business Projects to Sell, n.d.). The material is also considerably cheaper than other materials (such as fabrics, wood, etching, etc.) and takes much fewer resources such as time and electricity to produce. You can also create digital SVG vinyl artworks for customers to download and cut from their Cricut machines—which is a great idea considering that many of us have been home-bound due to the pandemic.

With vinyl, you can explore projects such as wall art, stickers, decals, and themed vinyl for special occasions such as parties or get-togethers for Christmas, Easter, etc.

Wedding decor has been a major point of interest for Cricut entrepreneurs as Pinterest recorded a spike in the search had gone up by 441%. Although weddings are a little tougher to cater to in our current conditions, creating decor for such occasions is still a factor to look into, as many customers are looking for more cheaper, customized pieces for their small get-togethers.

Leather has always been a topic of interest, considering how versatile of a material it is. If you are interested in the material and how it can be customized into different products, and your Cricut can handle cutting the material, you should look into creating leather products. It's extremely unique of a material and is still a niche market (for entrepreneurs), with a high demand for it from customers. You can start small, by creating pieces such as earrings and bracelets before tackling tougher projects.

Lastly, cards are the most versatile of products to offer with your Cricut, and you can use various materials to create them! It's also a great way to master your skillset with your machine, as you can start simple and then work your way up, creating more complex and unique cards to add to your catalog. They're always on demand and a fantastically handy little product to offer customers! Especially considering that many people send gifts to others via online stores, offering cards as a product on an online store (such as Etsy) can be an easy way for customers to make use of their service and find your product easily!

Mindset

The *most* important thing to create a mental habit of, when starting a business (especially with your Cricut) is to be realistic about your business plan. Being an entrepreneur can be one of the most rewarding feelings in the world because you're in charge of your business and working with something that you're extremely passionate about; however, taking on the role of an entrepreneur can be equally as risky and requires a lot of responsibility and deep, logical thinking when it comes to business moves.

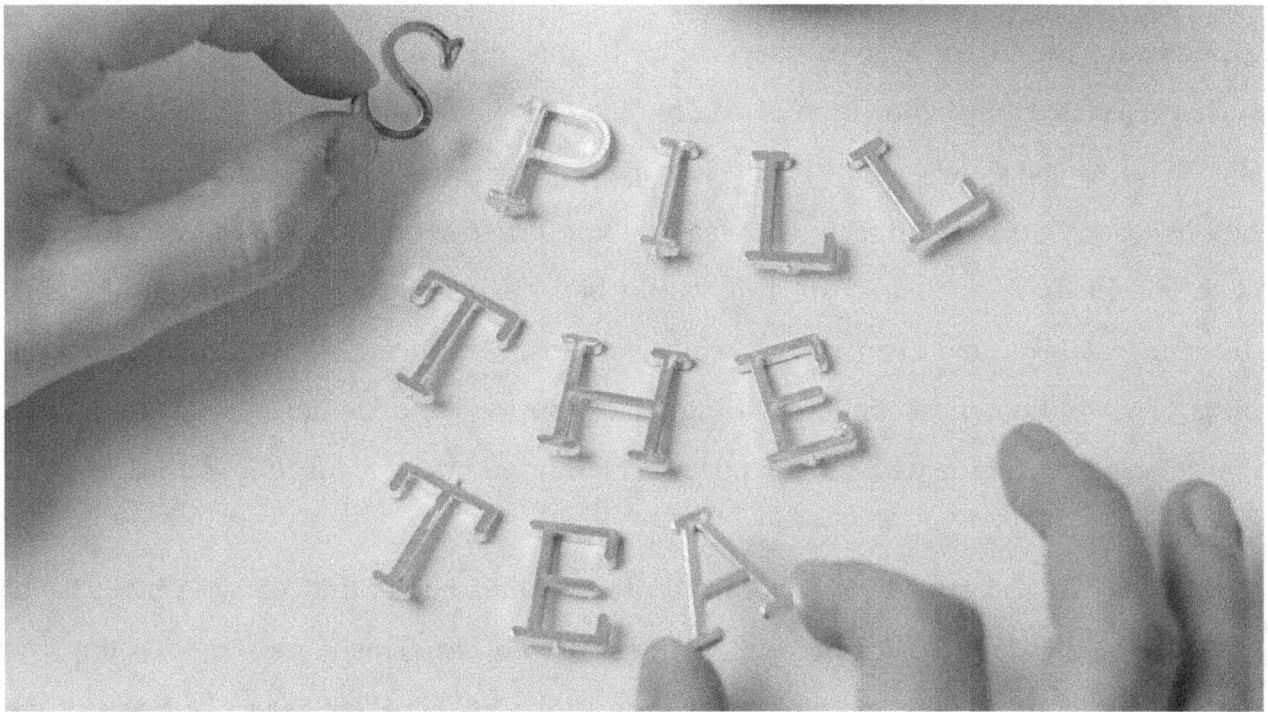

This is primarily because our emotions can sometimes get the better of us, especially because our business is much more personal. You should aim to ask yourself the harder-hitting questions such as: are you the right person to hold a successful business through its ups and downs? Can you efficiently problem solve, when placed under immense stress? Are you able to see projects through to their completion and not give up?

Aim to be brutally honest with yourself when asking these questions and look for inspiration and information to help guide you through what it takes to *mentally* and emotionally be a leader/business owner. If you are looking to start your business, the last thing you'd want to do is to risk losing money—so aim to ask yourself if you do truly have what it takes to work with your business from the foundations right through to its success.

There's also a new layer of risk involved because you have to manage your expenses to profits ratio and ensure that those requirements are met so that your business isn't incurring unfixable losses. For instance, you'll need to consider the expenses for the Cricut process - the cost of the machine, materials, and other resources such as electricity and your time! If you're new to the business world, you may want to start with an extremely small business with fewer products and few resources, then slowly work your way up from there so that you don't get overwhelmed with the flow of the business. A great idea for this would be to experiment with a few products in different catalogs, and then seeing which of those products sell well before making more. This is known as understanding your "supply and demand" market so that you're able to meet the demands of customers and not create a surplus of products that aren't selling well.

You can also start by developing processes and habits that you can stick to, to ensure that the daily basics of your business are sorted. This could be spending the morning replying to emails, and stock-taking in the evening, for example. Because we can't be motivated 24/7, we need to aim to be disciplined to ensure that we've been productive for our benefit.

You need to ensure that this business journey is enjoyable for you; if you're not enjoying running your business or making your products, then you're not going to be motivated and you won't be as efficient as your business requires you to be! Because being an entrepreneur is such a personal task and responsibility, you need to make it a fun and learning experience for you.

One of the most resourceful and easiest ways to achieve a successful company fueled with enjoyable experiences, full of lessons and profits, is to work on developing the mindset of an entrepreneur. You will need to not only assess your business plans, but also how motivated and passionate you are to see through the tougher periods (as every business will have its ups and downs)

Making Money with Cricut

Set Your Niche

Establishing your niche market can be quite tricky, but once you've got it right, it's quite easy to grow from that solid foundation! When determining your niche market, you need to ask questions such as: who will benefit from your product, what the general age and income levels of your target market is like (so that you can market and price your products accordingly), how will your market benefit from the product, what social media platforms or shops does your target market usually go to (to determine where to sell your products) and what are the locations of your niche markets. Asking these questions can help you specify your target market to help you create more customized products for them that are also affordable to them and easily accessible to them—without compromising your business' profitability, of course.

It's vitally important to establish a niche market, especially if you're a small business owner and/or have an online presence (through social media or a website). This is primarily because the market is so large and competitive, that you need to specify a unique product to a specific target market so that you're able to gain some attention and traction before building off of that. For instance, if you like making hanging mobiles that are space-themed, you may want to market your product to other space-geeks who enjoy marathoning space-venture movies, books, and novelty items. In doing so, you're creating a product that will get them excited to buy it, as they feel seen by your business.

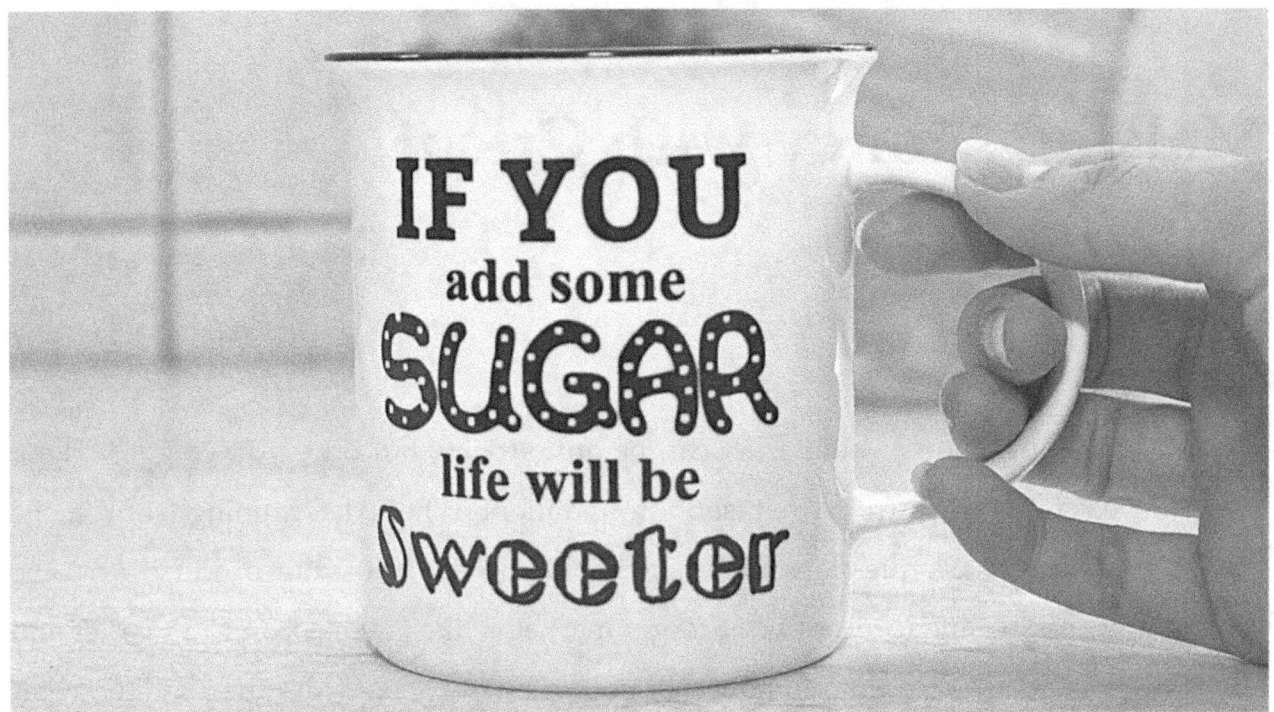

When establishing your niche, you will need to first create and offer a product that is unique to you and your business, that will stand out among its competitors. You'll need to also ensure that there will be a demand and use for the product—there's no point creating a product that will only benefit or interest you, then try to sell it to others who may not be interested. This will require extensive research into who you'd like to market your product to, around how much they will be willing to pay for your product, and of what use or interest it will be to them. Thereafter, you'll need to investigate the best ways to market your product to your niche market. For instance, there's no use marketing a product that's targeted at seniors, on social media. You may want to consider going to craft markets and slow markets to sell your products there, where you will have a much higher chance of selling to your market. Lastly, consider providing your customers with the best customer service in comparison to your competitors. You may also want to consider asking customers for their feedback on your products and service so that you can refine your business to better suit their experience with you and your business!

Running a successful Cricut business can also be summarized by one single action: networking! Networking is *key* for building a strong community, a market for your product and business, as well as expanding your business to work and learn from other businesses in a similar field! Networking is *the* most important factor to consider when marketing your business because business owners are not only focusing on selling their product, but they're also focusing on how to expand their overall business to become a powerful, self-sufficient, and successful company! Thankfully for you, the Cricut community is so large and diverse, so there are plenty of fellow Cricut entrepreneurs whom you can work with, talk to, and be inspired by. Try to find a few Cricut entrepreneurs that share more specific similarities to you, such as fellow Cricutters that are in your area or Cricut entrepreneurs who also make use of the same materials as you. You can also look for companies that work with Cricut business owners, for instance, if you make leather vase holders for flowers, you could contact flower boutiques or event planners in your area and keep them in your client books so that you can work with them in the future. Aim to expand your company's services by spotting other businesses/clients who can work with you, so that you can keep each other in mind when dealing with customers.

Building the Business

There are three key categories to consider in terms of creating a good and healthy flow of a successful business: the business' brand, the short-term, medium-term, and long-term goals of the business, and the business' networking opportunities. You need to aim to constantly reflect on these three categories to keep your business both grounded as well as growing. Try to assess these categories on a weekly or monthly basis so that you can ensure that your business is on track and on a stable line of growth.

One of the more cliché quotes in this chapter is the saying: work smarter, not harder. This sentiment pertains to the smaller, start-up businesses. As an entrepreneur, there are so many things that you have to do and remember on a day-to-day basis; there are so many responsibilities! With all that you have on your plate, why not lessen the load and find creative ways to work more efficiently?

Quality Over Quantity

Because entrepreneurs have such a personal relationship to their business and product, there's *much* more of an impact when the business owner interacts with customers (Hessinger, 2013). Humans love stories, and if your market isn't fully sold on your product, selling the product with a story of how you're the business owner and how you started your company will be more attractive to them. People want to be invested in products and by creating personal relationships with your customers, they'll more likely want to invest more into your story, journey, and product. So, in layman's terms, the first step in marketing your product or business is to put your best foot forward and reach out to potential customers.

Logically, as a small business owner, you will need to start small. Place more of your focus on the quality of your items and ensure that they are unique so that the customers that you do get, can wholeheartedly recommend your products to others. By creating a solid foundation of happy customers, you'll then be able to grow your market even further by word-of-mouth advertising (from your customers). As the orders come in, then you can work towards building stock.

You also need to understand the power of your brand and continue to evolve the brand and strengthen it, as you grow your business. As we mentioned above, you should aim to have your market cognitively associate certain symbols, colors, or products with your brand. If we look at a white tick, we associate this with Nike, and if we look at three diagonally white stripes, we associate this with Adidas. Similarly, you want to aim to have that same power with your brand. This power doesn't happen overnight, it happens slowly and evolves as your business grows, but it's important to have this vision at the start so that it can evolve naturally over time. Therefore, starting small will give you that room to play around and experiment with quality products that come with their unique stories, colors, names, etc.

Aim to refine your products and see how to set them apart from the competitive market. If you are selling your products online, there's a large opportunity for a greater market demand—which is great, as your product is exposed to much more potential buyers. However, there is also a plethora of other business owners and sellers online, with just as much passion and drive as you, to sell their products to your market. Online shopping has its perks: it's cheaper than renting out shops or stalls at markets, and it exposes your product to a much larger audience. But in doing so, there's also a greater rise in competition. To combat this, you'll need to create a brand and product that's unique and memorable to your audience. Try to create personal relationships with those who are interested in your product, and research the demographics of potential buyers so that you can expand your business in those markets. You have to be creative and driven regarding establishing your audience and expanding it.

Maintaining quality control should naturally come with running your business, but as things get busier and you add more to your plate, it does get tougher and tougher to ensure that you're spreading your energy over all the aspects of your business. Try to keep a checklist of basics that you need to get done in a day so that you don't compromise the quality of your product or customer service relations!

Admin Work (Costs and Savings)

Try to dedicate time weekly to assess the general production flow of your business and how you can better it so that you save on time and resources but still maintain the quality and quantity of your products. This sentiment ties in with the one brought up in the 'mindset' chapter, that as an entrepreneur, you should aim to constantly be problem-solving and improving. A more physical example of this is if you spend some time sifting through the prices of resources that you need on different websites so that you can find the cheapest options. You can also try to look at wholesalers for cheaper prices for your resources such as vinyl, materials, etc. to reduce your expenses and raise your profits! Many businesses aim to bulk buy their basic necessity resources so that they can cut costs on transport, etc.

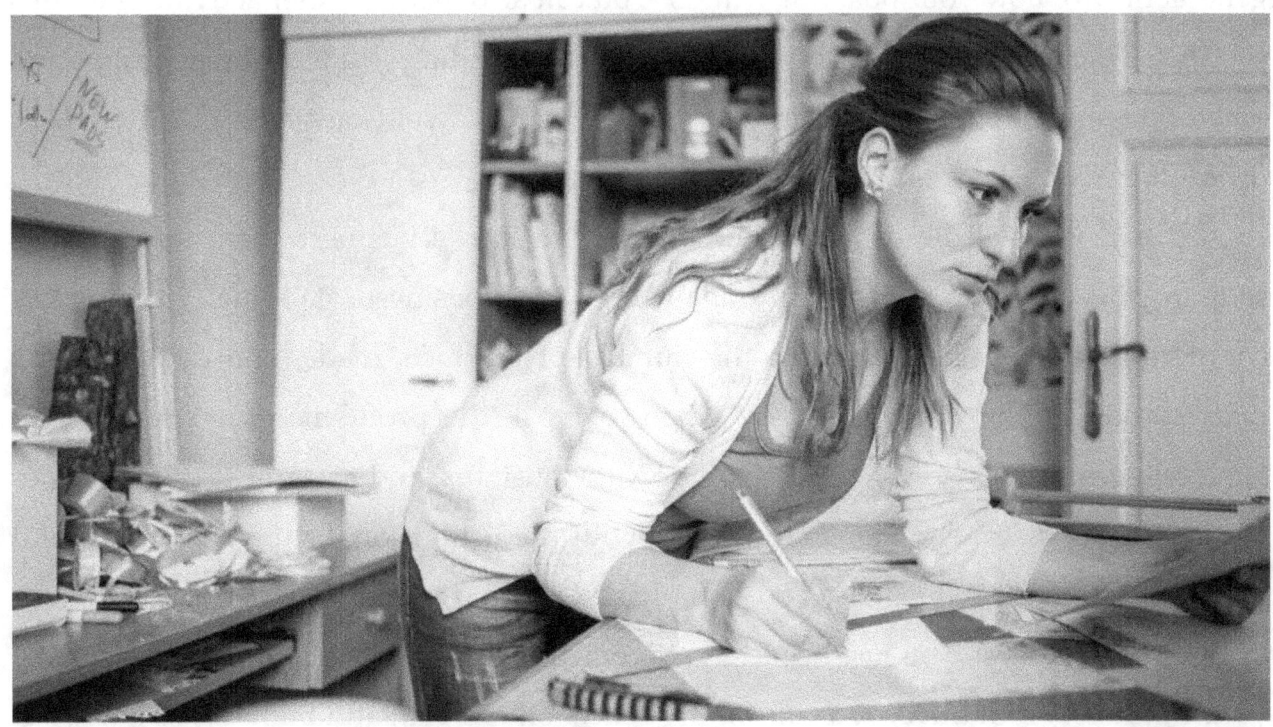

Another thing to consider is creating an emergency savings account for your business. If the pandemic has taught us anything, it's that times are extremely unpredictable, no matter how much we plan ahead. We always have to protect ourselves from those potentially uncertain times and risks of loss. Try to calculate your general costs for the next few months and set aside an amount that you'd like to save every month, in case your business incurs a loss.

Business Planning & Bulk Buying

Thereafter, think about the production process—from buying material and how much capital it will require, to making the products (and the expenses for resources such as electricity and time), to selling the products. This is your production cycle—the general flow of how your business will go. You can also include other activities into this production cycle such as replying to emails, spending time on marketing and networking, researching your market or industry, and travel times to fetch materials or drop-off parcels at clients or the courier.

Next, you will need to determine your company's business plan; this includes setting goals based on research and analyses of your business' standing. For instance, comparing your business' costs to the number of products made, and deciding how many products you need to sell by when to break the profit margin. You can also explore ideas such as how you'd like to grow the business, and add in research on other competitors or research on the industry and your predictions on the market (supply and demand) for your product, etc. You don't have to be too technical or serious with your business plan at first, you just need to jot down any goals and research that pertains to your business. From there, you can simply reflect on the plan and build off of it as your business builds, and you learn more about your company, the industry you're in, and most importantly, where your company stands in the industry that it's in.

Copyrights and Licensing

You may have to research the necessary licenses needed to sell your products online if you're an established business, as these laws do change by state. However, if you're a small enough business, you can get away with selling your products on social media sites such as Facebook Market or Instagram shopping. You may have to do a bit of research on your state's laws if you have an established website and are officially selling products with catalogs or offering a commission for Cricut projects.

Another extremely important thing to consider is that you need to be extremely careful with creating Cricut projects and their relation to logos or symbols of other brands. For instance, if you're making pillowcases for children's rooms, you may want to stray away from incorporating brands such as Mickey Mouse on the design and putting this online as your product. If you'd like to be safe, simply use the images, shapes, fonts, and designs that are offered by Cricut Access and manipulate those designs to your style and preference. It's a much safer route to go down and safeguards your business from any potential threats from other brands that you may have included in your designs. You will need to be careful about using licensed images, such as Disney characters, when creating products to sell. Stores such as Etsy won't allow you to sell your product on their site if you don't have the rights to such images.

Marketing

Thankfully, the internet and social media have *greatly* helped businesses regarding how they can market themselves. The development of online shopping (backed and accelerated by 2020's pandemic and urge to "stay at home") has positively altered the way businesses sell products from physical markets and stalls to online shopping.

Concerning platforms to sell your products, if you aren't already selling your products on your website or social media sites such as Facebook Marketplace (or your Facebook Page or a Facebook Group that you're a part of) and Instagram shop, you can also look into other considerably popular and trustworthy online shopping sites such as Etsy, Mercari, and eBay. You can also look into physically selling your product at craft fairs, farmer's markets, boutiques in your area, or simply by word-of-mouth via your friends and family. You can also look into joining Facebook groups or follow Instagram pages and hashtags that give tips for Cricutters who own businesses (Daher, n.d.).

The Cricut online community has such a strong online presence that they are constantly updating information for other Cricutters to use—whether it's project ideas, upcoming product releases by Cricut, or tips and tricks for fellow Cricutters and their businesses.

You can also follow these groups or join the communities to see what projects and products other Cricutters are selling so that you can make yours more unique to you. In addition to researching the competition and refining your product, you can also see how other Cricutters market their products online and what marketing strategies they use, and then try and test those marketing techniques out for yourself. You can make use of specific hashtags related to Cricut businesses to attract fellow Cricutters to your page. You can also post your product in Facebook groups that help promote small business owners' products; you'll just need to find Facebook groups in your area that are created to help business owners. For instance, certain Facebook groups are made for small, local business owners, and the admin posts updates on farmer's market openings, craft fair openings, etc. for business owners to book spots to sell their products. This changed due to the events in 2020, so the pages and groups have now expanded to allow business owners to advertise their products for others to see and share.

Another *extremely* helpful tool for your business is to create an online blog for your business and products because the online Cricut community is so large. Simply gathering a following on your blog can already open up the market greatly for your business!

There are so many options available to our disposal in terms of marketing our businesses nowadays, thanks to the internet and social media. By taking the time to refine your brand and products, it will be extremely beneficial for your business when marketing your products online. You can also work toward diversifying your online presence by marketing your product on numerous sites or pages so that your 'reach' for an audience is much larger.

Chapter 5: Project Ideas

Depending on your Cricut machine and the materials that it can tackle, there are so many options for projects that you can create to sell. You may also want to consider looking into your target market to see what other creations they may like.

For instance, if you want to look into just making cards using your Cricut Joy, you might also find it helpful to look into cutting vinyl for mugs, candles, and vases that could work well, hand-in-hand with a card as a gift for any occasion. In doing so, you can expand your brand from just selling cards to selling entire gift sets for any holiday, birthday, or celebration!

Cricut Joy

If you have the Cricut Joy, there are still a large number of projects that you can make to sell, even though the machine's capabilities are the most limited out of the entire range of models (Daher, n.d.). Here are a few project ideas for the Cricut Joy:

Personalized Cards

Selling personalized cards on stores like Etsy or being commissioned by others via your website. The Joy does shine its brightest in card cutting and making. With special materials such as the Joy's Card mat and pre-scored cards, it makes the production process of cards (with the Joy) that much easier. If you do make use of these tools and accessories for the Joy, you'll find that the card-making process is easier on the

Joy than on any other model!

You can keep your cards plain and simple, or you can jazz them up and create unique cards such as different shaped cards for different themes (i.e.. heart-shaped cards for Valentine's Day) or interactive cards such as spinner cards or pop-up cards.

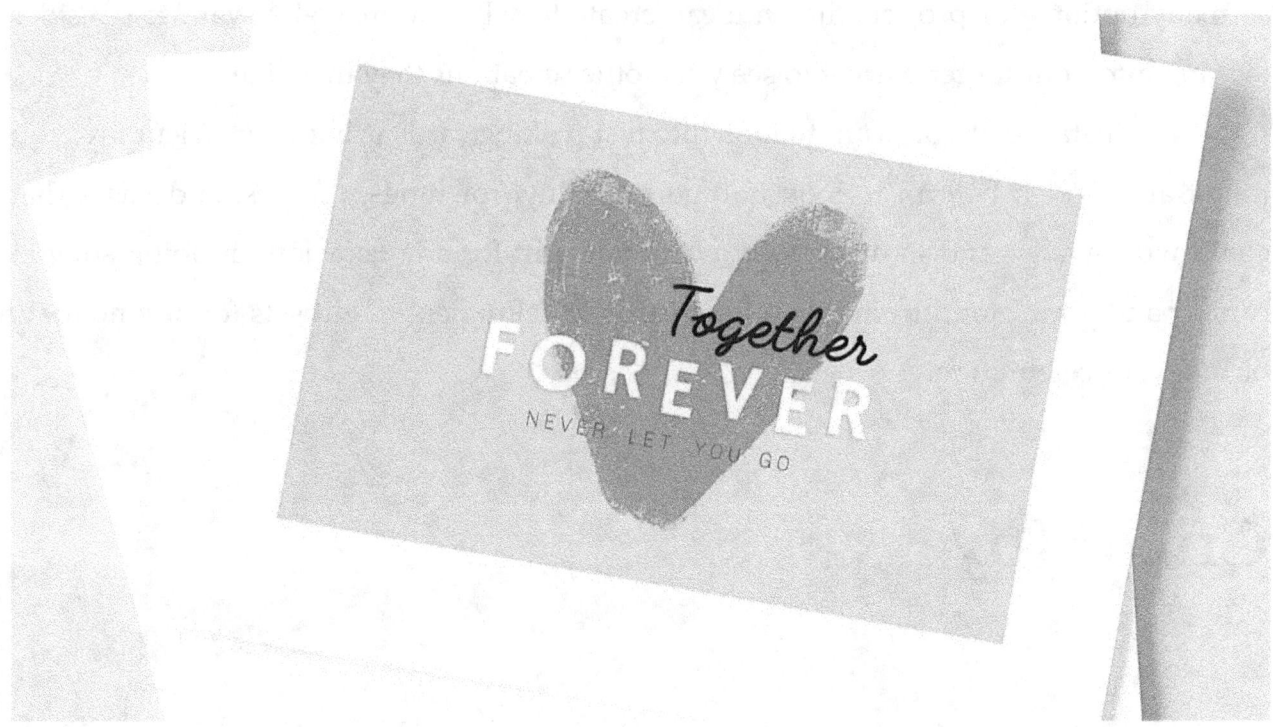

Personalized Vinyl Designs

Another great way to use your Joy machine is to create gorgeous vinyl designs (stick-on or iron-on) for project surfaces that can range from materials such as t-shirts to glassware such as mugs, vases, and candleholders. The reason why this is such a fantastic idea for the Joy is because of the Smart material range. Cricut created an entire iron-on and stick-on vinyl range and writable paper that is made specifically for the Joy. There's a large array of options to choose from, from different colors to their adhesive qualities (as some are permanent while others are removable vinyl). These are also a great way to personalize already existing pieces, such as mugs.

If you are familiar with Design Space (or any other illustration software) you can also design your range of artworks and images and upload the package to your website so that other Cricutters can buy it and incorporate your designs into their designs!

Personalized Bookmarks

If you love books and have a target market with an equal passion for them, you can also look into making personalized bookmarks! There are so many unique ways to personalize these and they're fantastic options for gifts! Not to mention, one can never have too many bookmarks, so you can constantly create new and unique bookmark ranges and sets! You can add in doodles or writing to make the piece more personalized and unique to your brand.

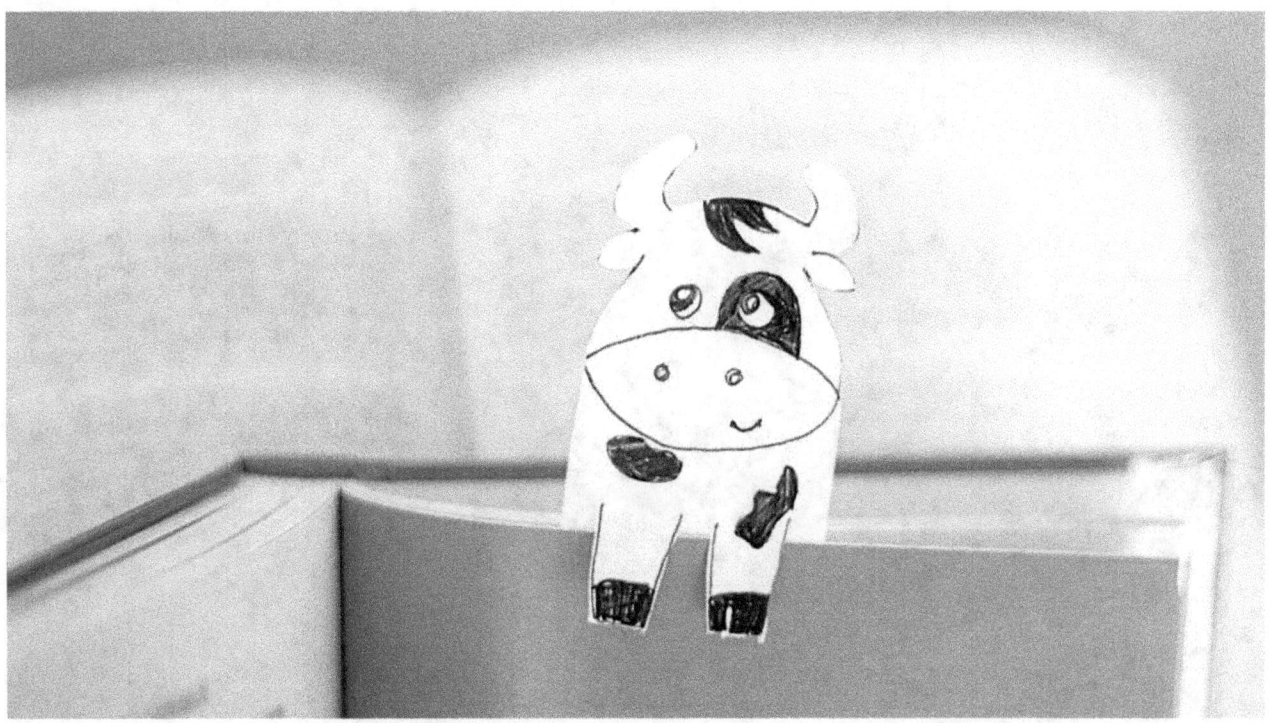

Cake Decorations

You can also pair up with party companies or cake companies to make gorgeous cupcake holders, cake toppers, and other cake-related decorations to make the most gorgeous and unique cake decorations for celebrations and special events!

Nail Art

Another fantastic collaboration option is to contact nail spas or nail technicians and offer to make them unique vinyl for their nail art (for their customers to choose from). This can also be a promising source of income if you manage to network enough and have a solid list of companies that you can collaborate with. Not to mention, you get to create stunning nail art for customers!

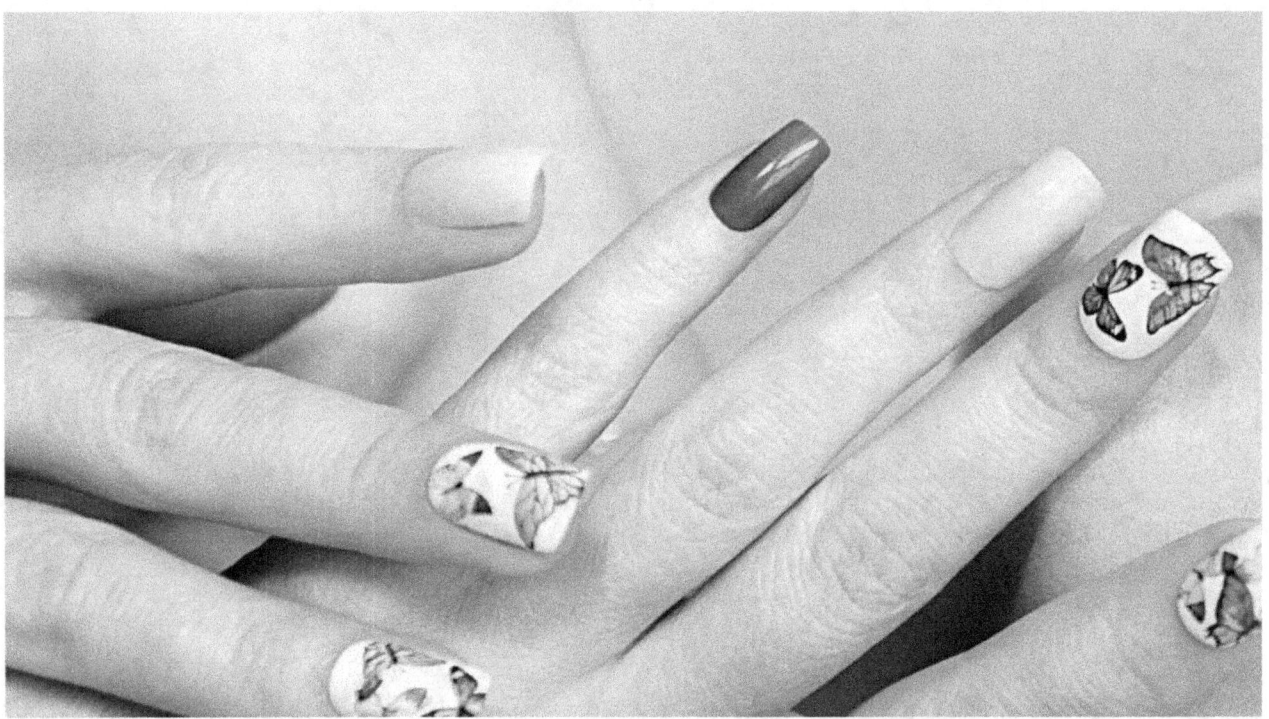

Garlands

One way that you can truly make the most out of the Joy model is to make paper garlands as wall decorations for parties and get-togethers. Because the Joy can tackle longer pieces of material at a time, it can be an extremely efficient way of cutting longer pieces of garlands in one go. You can either sell these online or at markets or team up with party and event companies to work with them and create paper decorations for events for their clients. The latter may be a promising option once events and get-togethers are allowed again, as it can be a stable and promising source of income.

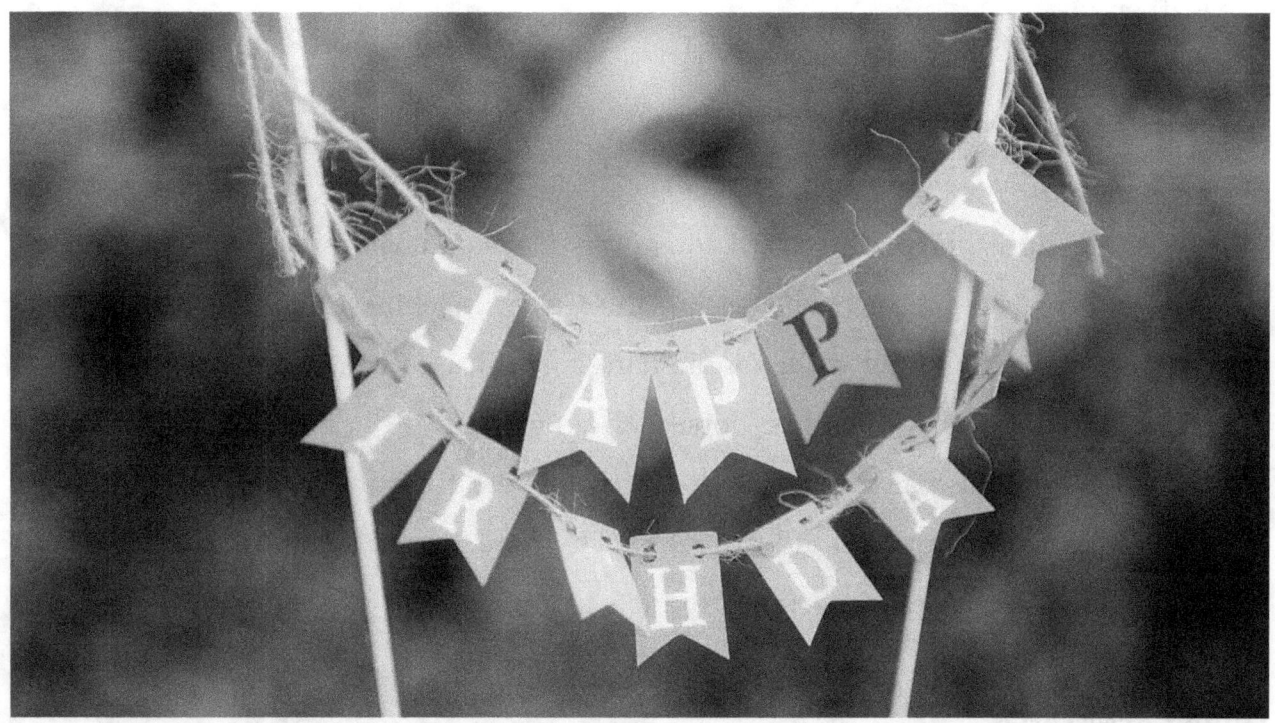

Cricut Maker and Explore Air 2

When we look at options that the Maker and the Explore Air 2 can tackle, we will consider both machines' abilities to take on these projects (mentioned below), because the Maker can essentially do what the Explore Air 2 does, and more.

The two machines do truly shine in tackling larger projects as well as cutting thicker materials than the Joy does, so one of the ways that you can make the most out of your machine is through cutting tougher materials such as wood and tough fabrics like leather.

Chipboard Decor

Cutting signs out of chipboard for home decor or businesses can be a fantastic and safe option as a product when using the Cricut machines, as these products are always in demand. Whether it's a simple hanging wall quote cut from chipboard or a sign for a restaurant, this can all be done with your Cricut! If you're able to work with other materials such as paints, varnishes, sandpaper, etc. to further customize the pieces, it will make it more unique and attract much more customers. You can also offer commission services for these sorts of products to attract more customers.

Dining Accessories

In keeping with the chipboard and wood theme, another handy and useful little product that you can make are coasters or placemats for the dining table. There are a few design options on Cricut Access for coaster patterns and templates that you can choose from, *and* Cricut also sells packs of plain, standard-sized coasters so that you can simply load them into your machine and cut designs into them with ease! Similarly, you can just adjust the measurements and dimensions of the coaster's patterns to placemats or potholders on the dining room table. These projects are not only easy to cut and make, but they are also extremely easy to customize and personalize, so you can make these projects unique to your business!

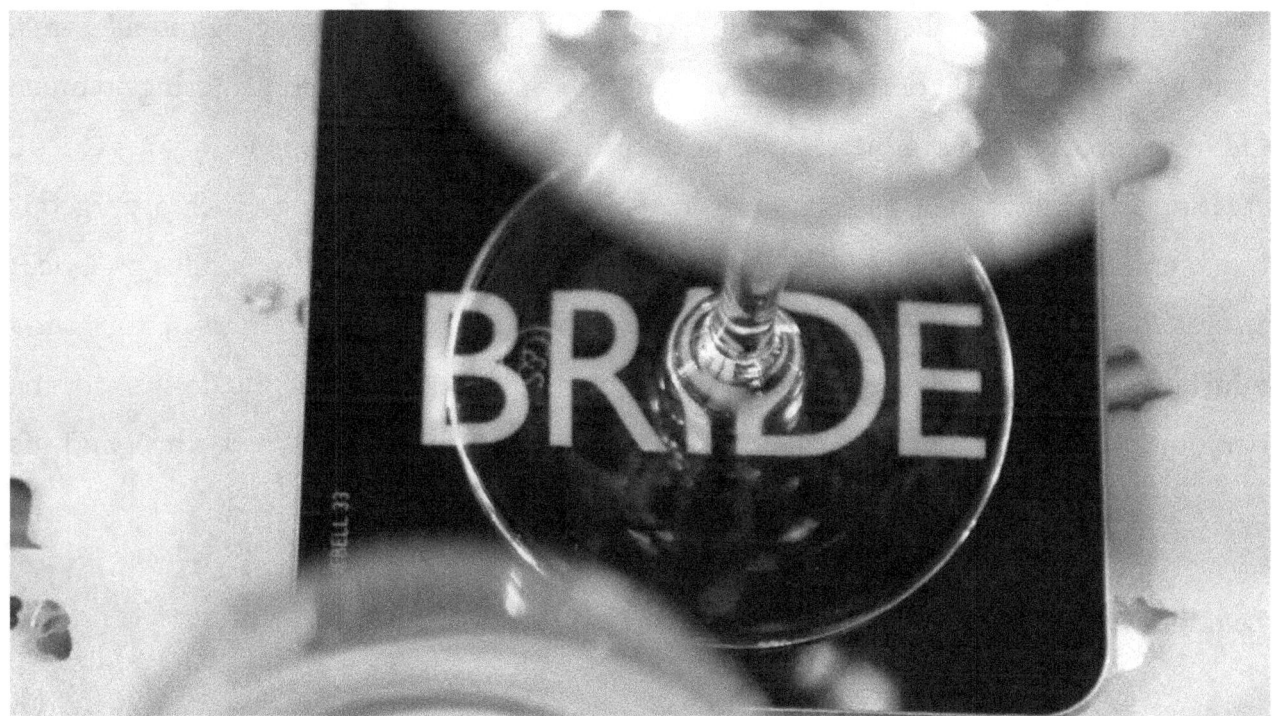

Wall Art

Considering that the Explore Air 2 and the Maker can both tackle much larger projects, you can explore different projects such as making gorgeous, eye-catching wall-art pieces for clients! If the design is much larger than the largest mat available, you can spread the design over multiple mats (in Design Space) and assemble the pieces. If you're feeling bold and confident enough to tackle such a large project, it's something that can help your business stand out among the crowd! You can explore patterns and quotes for wall-art as well, so there's an array of options and designs to explore! You can look into making mandalas as wall art, but in 3-D shapes so that it adds a lovely texture to a plain wall.

Hanging mobiles

In keeping with the idea of adding a bit of life into a room, hanging mobiles are a great way to bring a bit of natural movement into a boring room and can bring so much life to the space. If you're interested in exploring home décor options with your Cricut, creating hanging mobiles is such an easy project to tackle yet brings such a gorgeous touch and dynamic to spaces. There are a few templates for hanging mobiles on Cricut Access, but all you'll need for the project is a thread wheel, some string or rope, and whichever material you'd like to cut the hanging designs from. Once the designs for the hanging part are cut, you can easily assemble the pieces onto the thread wheel and it's good to go!

Leather accessories

Something that's become extremely popular with Cricut machines nowadays is leather projects—this is because leather is such a durable material and can be adapted and transformed into various products from accessories, to clothing, to accents for furniture, and so much more! If you're looking into exploring materials such as leather, you'll need to use the Maker for these types of materials (especially because the Maker has a few options for sewing as well, if you need any sewing done). One of the easiest points of starting and exploring how to tackle leather with your Maker is to work toward creating the smaller products first, such as accessories. Accessories such as earrings, bracelets, and belts are much simpler to create and are still such stunning pieces to add to your everyday look. They're neutral pieces that work with everything and add a touch of flare. By creating small accessories such as these, you can experiment with the material and how to work with it in Design Space, with the Maker and sewing it all together, while offering your customers gorgeous products in the end! Leather jewelry (and jewelry in general) does well on shops such as Etsy, so if you're looking into putting your products online, creating handmade jewelry (especially from leather) could make your business stand out!

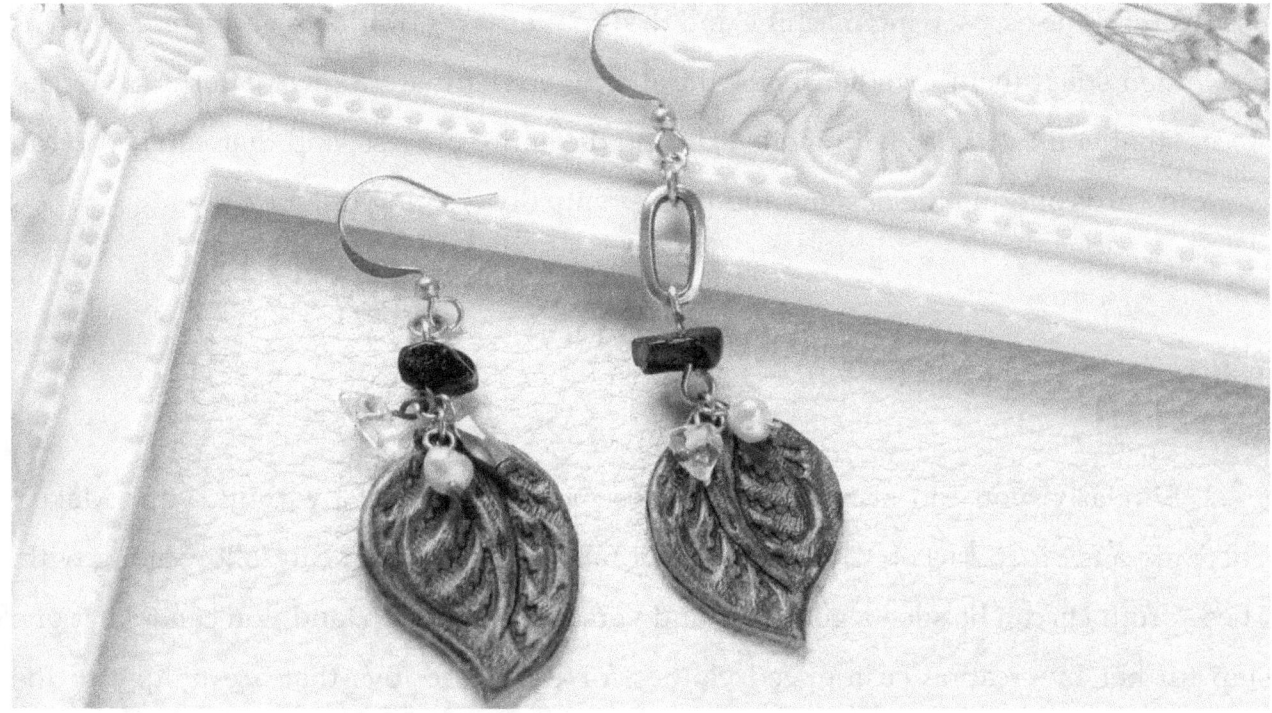

Clock faces

Something a little more unique and interesting to explore is creating analog clock faces! If you're interested in creating home décor related products to sell, you can also look into creating gorgeous and unique clock faces. You will need to grab the clock mechanism from a craft store, however, it's extremely easy to assemble! The clock face can be carved, cut, and printed on wood or chipboard, and then all you'll need to do is add in the clock's mechanism and it's good to go! It's a handy and unique little product to add to your catalog if you're interested in exploring the home décor field, and it's quite cheap to make and easy to assemble!

Outfit accessories

If you are looking to explore the capabilities of the Maker even further, you can use the machine as a sewing machine and draft patterns for outfits or accessories such as bags, then stitch them together using the machine. There are a few patterns on Cricut Access that you can work with while learning the entire process, and thereafter, you can work towards altering the designs and then eventually creating unique pieces!

Toys

Similarly, you can also make the most adorable fabric toys with your Maker! There are a few patterns on Cricut Access for fabric toys that you can follow along with. These products can be such a gorgeous and versatile gift option, and you can take it one step further by creating customized clothes for the fabric toys that are unique to the customer or event that's happening, you can charge more because it's a one-off product!

Pet accessories

As we've covered a few options from home décor to cake decorations and then to clothing, we can't forget the most important category in our lives: our pets! They deserve some love and appreciation too—and let's be real, pet parents *love* to spoil their pet-children, so creating a few adorable accessories for pets is a great way to attract more customers! Whether it's cutting gorgeous little collar bandanas for your dogs, or little fabric toys and balls for your pets to play with, the options for pet toys and accessories are endless!

Holiday decorations

Another way to challenge yourself and your capabilities with your Cricut is to imagine events or holiday get-togethers (or anything with a theme, such as a girl's spa night), and try to think about all the ways you could decorate or add to that event, just by using your Cricut machine to spice things up. For example, if it's a girl's spa night in and the theme is John Travolta movies (a promising theme), you can try to think about how you'd decorate the place with your Cricut machine. Maybe you could make a few garlands out of the word 'Grease' and lightning bolts and cut out a few face masks for a fun photo booth activity.

You can create a board game to go along with the theme of the night. In doing so, you've created an *entire* themed night, ready-made! You can use ideas like this as pack options for customers to order for their own themed events. The theme doesn't have to be that specific, it can be something more general and universal, such as Valentine's Day. However, using a unique theme for marketing purposes can help you boost your audience's attraction to your site. You can also offer the client an opportunity to come up with their own theme. You can then be commissioned to create items and decorations around the clients' theme for their event!

Whether your project ideas are small and intricate, such as creating nail art or earrings, or much larger business endeavors such as wall-art and decorations for themed events, the Cricut range truly promises to be a handy little, versatile, *and* powerful machine to help you along any of your ventures, whether it's simply to explore your creative side or to turn your projects into a full-blown, successful business venture! Try to look at the projects that you come across, whether it's online or on Cricut Access, and think about how you could make those items unique to your brand and style. By constantly challenging yourself to think outside the box, you're training your mind to find ways of making more unique, sellable products!

Also, try to constantly come up with creative ways to have your existing customers coming back for more. Whether this is in the form of offering discounts or loyalty points after every sale, try to find creative ways to keep your customers coming back for more. In doing so, you're also creating a more stable form of income with the existing clients that you have, and then you can work toward building off of that.

With so many fantastic opportunities offered by our Cricut machines, it is up to us to think creatively on how we want to approach the market with the tools that we have!

Chapter 6: Tips & Tricks for Your Cricut

Whether you plan to use the machine for personal projects or you plan to use the machine to create products, Cricut has developed the machine to be able to suit everyone's needs! It's so versatile to the point that the Maker can tackle over 300 types of materials, just so that there's a little something for everyone.

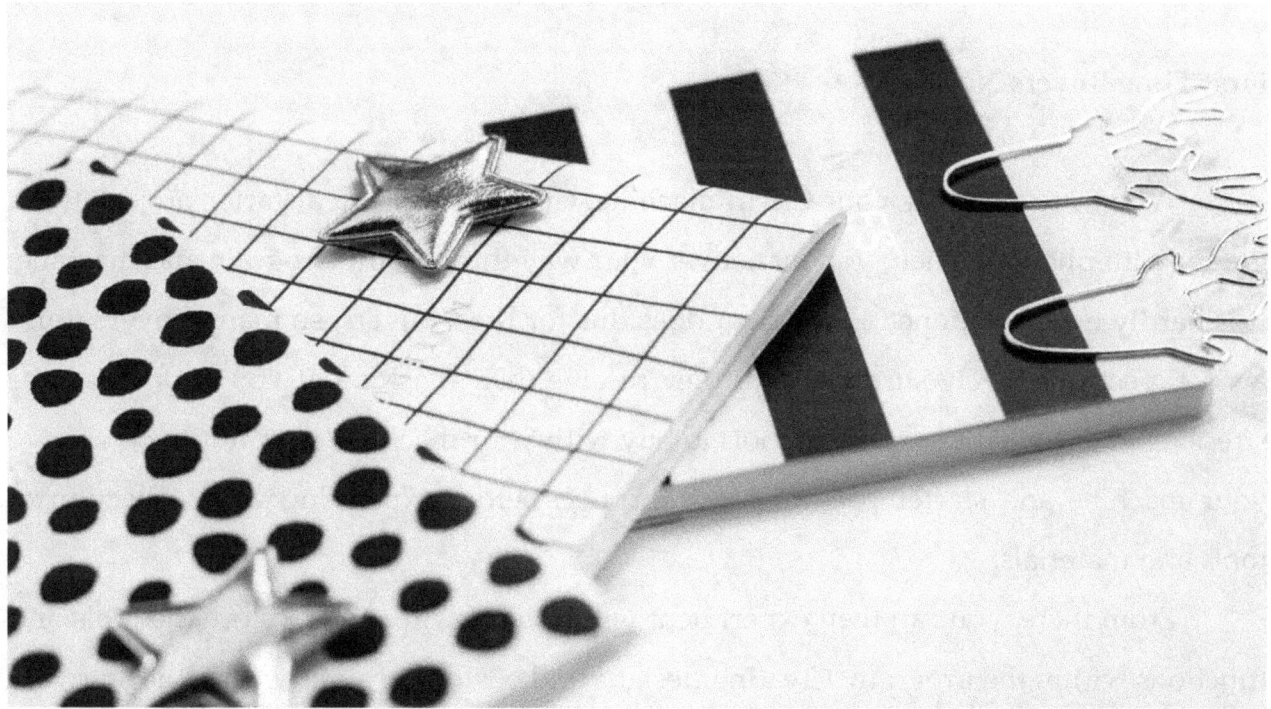

Now that we know of all the amazing benefits and capabilities of the machine and its software, there are a few final pointers to mention. The next few points which we are going to tackle are "frequently asked questions," insight on first buying the machine, and a few other handy tips for Cricutters.

Sharpening Your Cricut Blades

In short, the Cricut machines' major features are to cut, write, print and score. The Maker has expanded to be able to stitch as well, as it has a few settings for different stitches, however, you will need to buy these extra blades and accessories (Cricut Basics, 2018). If your blade becomes blunt., you can use aluminum foil to sharpen your blade. Scrunch up a bunch of aluminum foil to create a golf-sized ball, then simply poke the ball a few times with the blade until the blade sharpens. Using this technique can sharpen the blade without damaging the housing of the blade. Generally speaking, Cricut blades (that are used regularly) should be sharpened every 3-6 months.

First Time Buyers Notice

When you first buy your Cricut machine, Cricut sends you a starter project and a guide (with photos) to help you maneuver your way through the program and machine. It is hardly ever mentioned that Cricut does this for their buyers, so many buyers don't even expect this lovely surprise until they receive their machine. If you are hesitant or stressing about what materials or tools to buy with your machine, wait until you receive your machine and starter pack to work through before expanding your collection of tools and materials.

From there, you can then experiment with the software and explore the tools and functions within the program. Creating designs and custom projects within the software is pretty straightforward once you enter and explore the application. The interface is easy to use and understand, so you shouldn't have too much of a hassle maneuvering through the software. Try to keep it simple at first by creating easy designs so that you can get used to the general flow of Design Space and how it works with your Cricut, before moving onto creating custom designs and patterns.

In regards to what standard tools come with your machine when you buy it, you'll usually get a standard cutting blade and a cutting mat. The Explore Air 2, for instance, comes with the 12x12" StandardGrip cutting mat. Try to keep the cutting mat in its plastic case when you're not using it so that it doesn't pick up dust and lose its adhesiveness (Cricut Basics: Tools and Supplies, 2017).

The Maker's box comes with a rotary blade and drive housing, premium fine-point blade and housing, black fine point pen, fabric grip machine mat, light grip machine mat, welcome book, a USB cable and power adapter, free trial membership to Cricut Access, "50 free ready-to-make projects" inclusive of 25 sewing projects and a few materials for a practice project (Answering Your FAQs About the Cricut Maker, 2020).

You may want to consider getting a Deep Cut Blade if you want to cut through thicker materials such as chipboard or leather, as the standard blade that comes with the machine can only cut through materials such as paper and card stock. If you do want to work with various materials, you may also need to grab a set of cutting mats (they usually come in a variety pack of three). Try to get the three different grip mats, in different colors, so that you have options for adhesiveness, and you can work with a variety of materials.

For the Maker, you may consider wanting to get the Quick Swap Housing with Scoring Wheel at some point in time, as this tool is extremely helpful to swap through tools with ease. This tool is the only way you can get scored lines with the Maker, so if you want to make projects or patterns with scored lines, then you will need to consider grabbing this tool early on.

"Is Cricut Worth the Price?"

A lot of people also question whether their Cricut will be worth the money and if it truly is being put to good use. To answer this sentiment, it is all up to the Cricut owner whether the machine will be put to good use and worth its price. The Cricut range and capabilities are endless. From project ideas to tackling hundreds of materials, to having tools and accessories to tackle more projects, the Cricut models truly are as useful as you make them. There are endless possibilities for project ideas that can be used for your home, for gifting, or for selling. The choice is truly up to you in terms of how you use the machine.

Cricut was once just a machine for cutting cardstock and paper, but the company has truly made an extremely prominent effort to evolve the range to have multiple functions, capabilities, and tackle various materials. As the company grows, so will the models and their capabilities. One of the most notable factors is that the Cricut *does* require tools and accessories for other functions, but because Cricut gives you the standard machine with tools and a starter project to experiment with, you can decide what materials you'd like to use and tools you'd like to buy *after* working with the starter project.

When you want to expand your Cricut range and you're looking for tools and accessories to buy for your machine, there are a few factors to consider: your target market, your brand, and the materials that you're using.

There are a few aspects to consider before getting your Cricut machine, for instance, having a device that software such as Design Space can run off of. Also, if you are familiar with graphic design and illustrations, then you'll easily be able to create images without much hassle. However, if you aren't too familiar with graphic design and aren't too comfortable creating digital artwork just yet, then you can consider getting Cricut Access to assist you with options for images and options.

Considering that the machines are around $280, they are a bit on the pricey side, however, they do come with a lot of additional items such as the standard tools needed, practice materials, and free trials with project ideas. Cricut's website also runs promotions on machines and bundles with the machine; if you're lucky, you could grab a bundle for around $100 cheaper, so you just have to keep an eye out for any promos that they may be running. There are usually sales closer to holiday periods when they're clearing out stock or running specials.

Cleaning the Cricut Mat

When cleaning your mats, the best way to do so is to use a lint roller or cellophane tape to remove dust and debris from the mat, whilst maintaining its levels of stickiness. In doing so, you can lengthen the lifespan of your mat, so you don't have to buy another one every few months!

What Standard Tools Should You Get?

You will want to get a weeder, scraper, and scoring stylus (and scoring wheel if you're using the Maker). These are tools that will usually be used in most projects to help remove the design from the excess material, and securely adhere it to the project surface. You can use alternative tools such as tweezers in replacement of the weeder tool, and a credit card in replacement of a scraper; however, as you become more accustomed to your Cricut process, you'll want to have the proper assigned tools for the job.

Cricut does offer toolsets that contain all of the necessary tools for your machine, or you can purchase the bundles on the website, which offers the toolset with the machine. For example, the Essential Tool Set comes with a weeder, scraper, scoring stylus, tweezers, micro-tip scissors, a spatula, and a trimmer—these tools are the basic tools that you will need for most Cricut projects.

These options can be much cheaper than buying the tools individually. If you want to be extra fancy and spice up your working area, Cricut does make some toolsets that can come in the same color as your machine, so if you ordered a rose gold machine, you can get a matching rose gold toolset.

In addition to the toolset, you will need to consider what projects and materials you'd like to work with, with your Cricut machine. For instance, if you'd like to write or print on cardstock, you'll need a selection of blades to cut funky shapes and styles into your cardstock as well as a few pens for drawing. Some Cricutters say that they just buy pen holders from Walmart and a few Sharpies and it works perfectly fine. It also adds a bit more variety to the collection. Cricut does sell pens of all types and colors on their website too, so you have more than enough options for pens. If you are doing more intricate designs or have to do a professional project, you may want to use the Cricut pens for those projects and not other alternatives, as the Cricut pens are specialized to work with the machine on creating professional end products.

Working With Transfer Tape

You can also grab some transfer tape (which you can find on Cricut's website) which is used to help transfer designs from the mat to the project surface without damaging or distorting the design. Transfer tape can also be used multiple times, so you don't have to throw it away after every use. Transfer tape is also so handy regarding placing the design neatly onto the project surface and position it or readjust the placing of the design before adhering it onto the project surface.

If you don't have any Transfer Tape lying around, you can also use normal cling wrap as a transferring tool for your designs (and it's much cheaper).

Transfer tape is essentially a clear tape that you place the design onto once it's cut and then place it onto the project surface when you're ready to transfer the design over. Transfer tape also comes in handy when you're dealing with a lot of designs at once and need extra assistance to keep designs in place, while you weed some designs and adhere others to the project surfaces — it acts as a fantastic bridge in the process.

Familiarize Yourself With the Software

Learning to use and work with the Cricut machines is fairly easy, especially because Design Space does most of the work and instructs you on what to do when you're ready to use your machine. The biggest challenge with the Cricut process is to learn to work with Design Space. If you're not considerably tech-savvy, then you may want to spend some time adjusting to the software's layout and familiarizing yourself with the functions and processes. You can also try another software (like Inkscape) to see if you feel more comfortable with another layout or program. Keep a journal near you where you can jot down the shortcuts, functions, and processes that you need to follow for different projects so that you can just revert to the journal if you ever feel unsure of where to go or what to do in the software.

Conclusion

From discovering the capabilities of each machine to exploring the vast and beautiful world of Design Space, to the endless opportunities for gift options or creating products to sell, Cricut has made a unique and powerful machine that everyone can get something positive out of!

With Cricut's software and range of machines in combination with the potential market for Cricut-made products, we can honestly and whole-heartedly commend Cricut on expanding in unimaginable yet powerful ways.

The machine and brand have truly opened up so many doors of opportunities for creatives. It has allowed creatives the opportunity to create *and* work in a market that's so supportive. It places creatives in a community and market that's constantly promoting growth and professionalism. Cricut's brand has pushed its owners to not only explore their creative side but to also explore these creative sides *in consideration of* how it can evolve into a profession. Cricut has pushed us to tackle challenges, learn about our crafts, learn how to use technology to make our craft more efficient and current, as well as urging us to learn how to take these crafts into a professional setting and profit from the products made.

The biggest debate with most FAQs from the online Cricut community is the question of: is the Cricut machine worth its price? (Answering Your FAQs About the Cricut Maker, 2020). Simply put, Cricut doesn't need to be seen as a purchase if you don't want it to be one; you can make your Cricut machine an investment, it's all up to you! The opportunities that the Cricut machine offers are *endless*, but it's up to you to determine how worthwhile the machine is going to be for you.

You need to find ways to use the Cricut machine to your advantage. Aim to question what products or themes you are into, and how can you use your Cricut machine to learn more about the process of making them. As we covered in chapter 4 (about making money with your Cricut), there needs to be a level of passion and a desire to constantly learn and better your craft. If it's not enjoyable, it won't be successful—as with anything in life!

Take your time to explore your interests and then look into how your Cricut companion can help you explore your interests even further! Try to also establish a good Cricut community (whether it's online or in person) so you can share this common interest with others, and then share ideas and handy tips and tricks with each other.

Nonetheless, it's always great to have another option for a side hustle, and as you start delving deeper into your craft with Cricut, you may as well make some money from it! And, if anything, you'll be saving money by making projects instead of spending it on buying pre-made ones. As you delve deeper into the Cricut world, you'll also start to notice how inspired you'll become to try more projects with Cricut—especially because the list of project ideas is endless.

For the amount of joy, learning, and bettering a skillset, the Cricut machines are worth the buy. Now it's all up to you to decide on how you'd like to make use of your newfound friend!

If you liked this book or you have found an inspiration here, please leave us a review on Amazon. We appreciate every single feedback. It won´t take you too much time and it will help us a lot.

Thank you very much and wish you lots of creativity and success with your Cricut machine!